ACCELERATED PROGRAMS FOR THE GIFTED MUSIC STUDENT

ACCELERATED PROGRAMS
FOR THE GIFTED
MUSIC STUDENT

Paul Jankowski
and
Frances Jankowski

PARKER PUBLISHING COMPANY, INC.   West Nyack, N.Y.

Library of Congress Cataloging in Publication Data

Jankowski, Paul,
    Accelerated programs for the gifted music student.

    Includes bibliographical references.
    1. School music--Instruction and study--United
States. 2. Gifted children--Education--United
States. I. Jankowski, Frances,   joint
author. II. Title.
MT3.U5J3   780!.72973   75-12727
ISBN 0-13-000-943-1

Dedicated to

Our children, *Dawn, Kevin, Todd and Roger*
Our parents, *Mr. and Mrs. Paul Jankowski Sr., Mr. and Mrs. Louis
J. Kasprak*
Our uncle, *Joseph Jankowski*

A Word from the Authors on the Practical Value of This Book

Busy music educators are frequently tempted to skip through book introductions and plunge immediately into the body of the book. This procedure would be highly detrimental to the success of these programs for the gifted because each program is structured for gifted-divergent and/or gifted-convergent musicians. A degree of acceleration is developed proportionately to the proper direction of a program that best fits a particular student's thought process. For example, if low-creative students with high I.Q. scores were directed into the program for writing football half-time shows or composing music, the results would be noticeably unsatisfactory, since this segment is designed for the high-creative, divergent thinker.

We do not mean to imply that high I.Q. students should not write shows or be discouraged from using this program. It is merely desirable that the teacher realize acceleration and proper feed-back occurs only when the program fits the student. Therefore, it must be emphasized that "gifted music students," as used in this book, may fall into one or a combination of three categories:

1. High and above average creatives
2. Students who show leadership and an A or B grade in Ear-Training and/or other music courses
3. I.Q. of 115 or over

High and above average creative students have been placed first for a very definite reason. Identification of these particular music students transcends traditional classification and helps to select those who may have been slowed because of social, cultural, educational or verbal deprivation. Using the non-verbal Torrance Test of Creativity reduces the structured drawbacks experienced by migrant, ghetto or bi-lingual students, and it further helps identify students who may not have performed well musically due to economic or social limitations.

For the music educator who lacks testing time but desires to identify specific characteristics of the gifted-creative student, selected research has been presented in Chapters 1 and 2. To obtain the maximum accuracy and success of these programs, it would be best to follow the particular suggestions of each chapter.

After identification, students can be guided to develop skills for enriching existing music programs or beginning new ones. Often when these programs are presented to superintendents and school boards, a government title program or added funds can be obtained to subsidize the teaching of music during the summer months or within the school year.

Good music educators have voiced a concern about the complexities of our society and the need for identifying with and understanding today's students. Due to the large number of music students in a classroom situation, teachers cannot always reach and guide an individual. Some students may be extremely talented musically but are difficult to handle in a disciplined situation. The need for helping students before they become problem adults appears paramount. But what can an overworked music director do to develop better understanding in a limited time? Some thoughts can be analyzed with the Torrance test. Unlike achievement, I.Q. or musical performance tests, it reveals potential creativeness and helps determine which students should write music, which half-time shows and which should teach the technique of musical production and ear-training.

Gifted students can write refreshing half-time shows. This does not mean simple mechanical charting or instrument placement, but contemporary creative ideas presented by students for entirely new shows. This can be very rewarding and a great help in accomplishing the continual task of half-time preparation. Material lists, methods for guiding gifted music students to write shows themselves, and a series of show suggestions can be found in

Chapter 3. The program is structured for individual independent development with a minimum of controlled supervision.

In Chapter 7 it is suggested that music classes be extended beyond the music department to non-music students. Art, English or social studies teachers can devise a slide-lecture program to coordinate a special period in history. Students receive positive scholastic feedback from peer groups with such academic exposure. Gifted students can be trained to present an interesting audio-visual coordinated presentation by following the outline and procedure suggested in Chapter 4. This projected teaching can be accomplished during regular music appreciation classes or as an independent study program.

A folk-jazz club can be an effective part of the music curriculum. An approach such as this draws in the minority groups within a high school. Resource people in the community could be used as para-professionals to teach this particular group of students.

The variables in obtaining proper intonation for any music performance group are almost endless. A workbook section—Part 4—has been structured to deal with this complex problem. By training the gifted to tune individual instruments and a band, they not only improve their own ear but assist in tuning a large group of musicians.

Some of the most extensive ideas are found in the "Comparative Arts" program. Those in the music field have often mentioned how narrow and specialized music can be. However, students can broaden their concept of world evolvement through such a course as this. The technique is to use musical figures in the context of world history with ample use of charts, slides and student lecturers.

Elaboration and theory have been avoided in developing these programs. Research has proven over and over again that it is not the method but the teacher that brings success to the curriculum. It is our sincerest hope that this book will prove to be a perfected tool in skillful hands.

Paul and Frances Jankowski

Contents

A Word from the Authors, About the Practical Value of This
Book . 7

PART 1. IDENTIFICATION OF GIFTED MUSIC STUDENTS . 17

Chapter 1. Distinctive Characteristics of the Gifted-Creative
          Student . 19

A. Introduction
B. I.Q. and Achievement
C. Underachievement
D. Temperament and Vocation
E. Anxiety
F. Reading Preferences
G. Sense of Humor

Chapter 2. Analyzation and Testing Students for Gifted
          Programs . 30

A. Testing Method and Procedure
B. Dialogue for Testing
C. Grading Tests and Avoiding Pitfalls
D. Preparing Charts for Analysis
E. Chart Summation

PART 2. INDIVIDUALIZED PROGRAMS FOR DEVELOPING
       GIFTED MUSIC STUDENTS . 47

Chapter 3. Training Gifted Music Students to Write Half-Time
          Shows . 49

A. Introduction
B. Scheduling

Chapter 3. Training Gifted Music Students to Write Half-Time
           Shows (cont.)

C. Psychological Encouragement
D. Booklist
E. Duration
F. Half-time Flash
G. Guidelines, Checklists, Tape Recorder Use, Student Worksheet
H. Video Tape Analysis and Playback

Chapter 4. Using Gifted Students in a Multi-Media Approach to
           Music Appreciation Class   . 66

A. Telescopic Curriculum
B. Tape Carrel Use
C. Use and Analysis of Charts
D. Slide Preparation
E. Script Preparation and Presentation
F. Critical Analysis with worksheets

Chapter 5. Placing Gifted Students in a Folk-Jazz Club   .   82

A. Avoiding Pitfalls
B. Definition
C. Club Forms
D. Administrative Questions
E. Instructor Application Form
F. Monetary Compensation
G. Use of Audio-Visual Aids

Chapter 6. Advancing Gifted Students in Music Theory .   99

A. Tests
B. Directional Teaching
C. Ear Training
D. Supplemental Study
E. Rap Sessions
F. Written Critiques

Chapter 7. Comparative Arts Course for Gifted Music Students
           . 117

A. Selections of Arts Figures, Events and Inventions

Chapter 7. Comparative Arts Course for Gifted Music Students (cont.)

B. Lists
   1. Architects
   2. Composers
   3. Dramatists, Novelists, Poets
   4. Painters
   5. Sculptures
   6. World Events and Inventions
C. Preparing Arts Notebook
D. Guidelines and Question Sheets
E. Outlines
F. Lecture with Audio, Visual Samples
G. Record List

**Chapter 8. Independent Guitar Study for Gifted Music Students
    . 139**

A. Question Sheet
B. Introduction to Music and Guitar
C. Questions and Answers
D. Supplement to Teaching Guitar
E. Supplemental Materials List

**PART 3. SELF-DIRECTED PROGRAMS FOR GIFTED MUSIC
    STUDENTS   . 151**

Chapter 9. Choosing Student Teachers   . 153

A. Selection Procedure
B. Using Cassettes
C. Overview of Preparedness
D. Character Analysis

Chapter 10. Controls for Gifted Student Instructors   . 161

A. Administration of Student Instructors
B. Role Playing
C. Progress Reports
D. Fees
E. Evaluation and Continuance
F. Instructor Improvement

Chapter 11. Placing Student Instructors   .   **170**

A. *Feeder School Questionnaire*
B. *Private Instructor List*
C. *Charting a Town*
D. *Problems and Handling Procedure*
E. *Parental and Student Feedback*

Chapter 12. Teaching Gifted Students to Test and Tune Individual Instruments   .   **177**

A. *Testing for Individual Variables in the Instrument*
B. *Tuning and Maintenance of the Clarinet*
C. *Tuning and Maintenance of the Cornet, Basses, Single Horns*
D. *Tuning and Maintenance of the Bassoon*
E. *Tuning and Maintenance of the Percussion Section*
F. *Tuning and Maintenance of the French Horn*
G. *Tuning and Maintenance of the Flute and Piccolo*
H. *Tuning and Maintenance of the Oboe*
I. *Tuning and Maintenance of the Saxophone*

Chapter 13. Gifted Students Tuning a Band   .   **190**

A. *Questions, Answers, Step Progression*
B. *Pyramid Tuning*
C. *Author's Method*
D. *Stroboscope*
E. *Tuning Bar and Piano Method*
F. *Video Taping*
G. *Teaching Small Ensembles*

Chapter 14. Awareness of Deception in Intonation for Gifted Music Students   .   **198**

A. *Temperature Changes and Its Effects*
B. *Traditional Standards*
C. *Breath Affects*
D. *Statistical Standards*
E. *Course of Action*
F. *Summary*
G. *Ear Pollution*

Index   .   **205**

ACCELERATED PROGRAMS FOR THE GIFTED MUSIC STUDENT

Part 1

IDENTIFYING GIFTED
MUSIC STUDENTS

CHAPTER 1

Distinctive Characteristics of the Gifted-Creative Student

A key to the use of programs outlined in this book is proper identification of the student to be considered "gifted." Students may easily be identified by experienced music educators if they fit comfortably into one or a combination of categories; solo or first chair performers, leadership with a B grade in Ear-Training, Theory or other music courses, an I.Q. of 115 or over.

But what of the migrant, ghetto or immigrant student who due to cultural deprivation does not fall into any of the above categories? Since our school is located between Chicago to the north and the steel mill city of Gary, Indiana, to the east, we have a natural influx of such a diverse student population. The added challenge of accurate communication with these students has long been an interesting controversial debate. The answer, in part, to give the students an enriched experience of a gifted program, is to identify these students beyond the categories used in the past. Try to identify these students for Creativity. The high and above average creative is the first measurement of gifted identification. It holds first position because we have found it excellent for all students regardless of background but especially helpful with minorities. Creativity identification takes us up the pathway of divergent thinking and opens up new areas of consideration beyond the normal strains of I.Q., achievement or performance.

Should you find yourself limited in time to properly test this area, then it is well to attempt classification through verbal questioning. What is the definition of creativity? What is the temperament of the creative? How well do they achieve? Does I.Q. make a difference? Does socioeconomic or parental approval have an influence? If you have failed to answer these questions, then you will find the capsule accumulation of research in the following pages quite helpful in recognizing characteristics of creatives. We strongly recommend however, that you test these students as soon as possible for more complete and accurate identification.

DEFINITION

Paul Torrance gives us a workable definition of creativity as the process of becoming sensitive to problems, deficiencies, gaps in knowledge, missing elements, disharmonies; identifying the difficulty; searching for solutions, making guesses, or formulating hypotheses about the deficiencies; testing and retesting these hypotheses and possibly modifying and retesting them; and finally communicating the results.[1] From the general pattern of Creativity we must step into the specific characteristics of a creative student.

I.Q. AND ACHIEVEMENT

Although previous research has indicated that I.Q. and creativity are each related to academic achievement and are relatively independent of each other, the results of certain studies question this relationship. The Cicirelli study investigated the I.Q. level at which creativity begins to affect achievement.

Results showed there was significant interaction between I.Q. and creativity which affects the arithmetic achievement only. Beyond a certain I.Q. additional I.Q. will not distinguish individuals in terms of academic achievement. No maximum I.Q. threshholds were found for reading or arithmetic achievement in terms of creativity. There was a maximum I.Q. level of 130-139 in which language success affected language achievement. Graphs of achievement showed an increase of achievement with I.Q. level up to 130, where an apparent plateau in achievement began. There was no certain I.Q. level creativity would distinguish individuals in terms of academic achievement. There were no minimum thresh-holds within a critical I.Q. and creativity distinguishing individuals in terms of academic achievement. Results of the study offer little support to confirm Anderson's ability-gradient theory in which I.Q. would have no effect on achievement, but creativity would begin to have an effect. There was a weak relationship between creativity and achievement.[2]

Edwards, Meredity and Tyler found success with creativity is not related to school achievement but with S.C.A.T. test. General scholastic aptitude abilities in intelligence tests cannot measure high creative abilities. Relationships of comparing creative scores and academic achievement is very limited. More of these tests need to be given in a consistent manner to set up a consistent pattern for clarity. S.C.A.T. test is better test for school achievement than creativity. High correlation on tests was found between I.Q. and achievement tests. There was an extremely low correlation between I.Q. and creativity index. The validity of creativity is questionable. Below 120 I.Q. determined achievement closely, while above 120 I.Q. is more closely related to creativity.[3]

Scholastic aptitude measures and high school rank do not show significant relationships to the quantity or quality measures of creativity. According to Skager, Schultz, and Klein, socioeconomic status showed no significant relationship to the quantity or quality measures of creativity. However, the quantity measure does appear to relate more highly to quality for a technical institution, there still appears to be no difference in the case of a state university. Within the two institutions there was a zero relationship between SAT scores and high school rank. There was a negative correlation between socioeconomic status and high school rank.

The failure to find a significant relationship between scholastic aptitude and high school rank is due to the tendency for a college admission to balance high school rank against aptitude scores in selecting students. Secondary school grades, although used for measurement for college entrance are not a standard continuum. The measure of quality of creative activities appears to be more influenced by scholastic aptitude, while quantity measures creative activities is more dependent upon intellectualized home atmo-sphere. Quantity and quality appeared positively correlated when-ever tested.[4]

In December of 1963, the Lorge-Thorndike Intelligence Tests and the Iowa Tests of Educational development were administered to all students in the ninth and eleventh grades of a laboratory high school. In addition, a battery of the Minnesota tests of creative thinking was given and a total creativity score was derived by the scheme suggested by Yamamoto.

Complete results were available for 75 ninth-grade (42 boys, 33 girls) and 84 eleventh-grade (43 boys-41 girls) students. Findings were as follows:

1. In the ninth grade, the correlation between IQ and creativity .12 and it was -.01 in the eleventh grade, neither being statistically significant.

2. The linear correlations between achievement measures and IQ was all significant and ranged from .63 to .73 in the ninth grade and from .62 to .86 in the eleventh grade.

3. Those between achievement and creativity were quite low in both grades and only background in social studies in the ninth grade approached the level of statistical significance.

4. Creativity means of the overachievers and underachievers did not show any consistent trend across the different achievement areas to favor either one of these two groups.

5. In the ninth grade, the overachieving groups obtained a higher mean creativity score on six of the nine achievement subtests.

6. In the eleventh grade they recorded a higher mean on four subtests.

7. In none of the nine areas of achievement did the difference in means of the two groups reach the level of statistical significance.

8. Because of the low IQ-creativity and achievement-creativity correlations, the results of analyses of covariance were essentially the same as those of analyses of variance.

9. The comparisons between the means seemed to favor the underachievers rather than the overachievers.

10. There was no evidence in this particular subject group to indicate that over-achievers are more creative than underachievers in any of the subject matters.[5]

An excellent source of information about productivity is Terman. After identifying children with IQ's of 140 and higher in the early 1920's Terman made several follow up studies. When the males in the group were twenty-five years or older 150 were rated highest in success as measured by productivity (not income) and 150 were rated lowest were then compared on a number of items that had been gathered from their childhood. During the elementary school years the high and low success group had been much alike, having about the same grades and tested achievements. Early in high school the groups began to draw apart, the success group getting higher grades. A far greater percent of the successful adult group had finished college. The most spectacular differences showed up between the two groups in 1940 when they were 25 years old or older. The productive group, far more than the less productive group, was superior in these personality characteristics; persistence in the accomplishment of ends, integration towards goals as contrasted to drifting, self-confidence, and freedom from inferiority feelings. The successful group appeared to have a much stronger drive to achieve good all-around mental and social adjustments and was relatively free from severe emotional tensions that bordered on the abnormal. Terman concluded that productive achievements and IQ are far from perfectly correlated, just as Guilford, Drevdahl and others have more recently concluded.[6]

UNDERACHIEVEMENT

The purpose of the investigation by Wonderly and Fleming was to evaluate the relative emotional adjustment and personality characteristics of achieving and underachieving intelligent creative children.

RESULTS

1. The results suggested that underachieving intelligent creative children were no better or less well adjusted than achieving intelligent creative children.

2. The underachieving intelligent creative in spite of being subjected to criticism by parents and teachers for not performing as well as they might did not get depressed or become dissatisfied with self as demonstrated by the self-rating scale.

3. There was no loss of status or acceptance by peers because of underachieving of the intelligent creative.

4. No significant difference could be discovered in any of the thirteen areas investigated. This would suggest an underachieving intelligent creative child does not develop particular personality types as a result of achievement level.

5. Creative children with certain kinds of personality traits do not become underachievers.

6. Arguments based on the effect of such pressures on academic achievement in underachieving creative children are also without foundation. Underachievers are not affected emotionally either through pressures for academic achievement or from those educators who demand more rigid requirements from these children.

7. The study supports the theories of Getzels and Jackson who feel that creative children prefer risk situations. [7]

TEMPERAMENT AND VOCATION

Bonsall and Gallagher compiled information of 1,359 white high school senior boys in several high schools in metropolitan area after they completed SRA tests, the Guilford-Zimmerman Temperament Survey and gave enough information about themselves, occupation of their wage earning parent to enable the occupation to be classified according to Alba Edwards Scale.

1. Gifted boys whose fathers were classed as professionals manifest greater objectivity at the 1% level when compared to non-gifted boys having professional fathers.

2. Gifted boys from homes where fathers are in managerial or clerical positions demonstrate more restraint at the 1% and 5% level than do non-gifted boys from like occupational backgrounds.

3. Gifted boys from homes where the fathers are in managerial jobs are at the 1% level more thoughtful than the boys from like homes.

4. Boys classified as gifted, whose fathers were employed in semiskilled and skilled occupations reveal more masculinity at the 1% and 5% levels than did average ability boys whose father's are working at similar jobs.

5. When gifted boys are compared with all other boys with the occupational levels of the home disregarded, they show at the 1% level more thoughtfulness and at the 5% level more general activity, restraint, emotional stability, objectivity and masculinity.

6. There were no significant differences between the total gifted and the total average students on the traits of sociability, friendliness and personal cooperation.

7. This study indicates that the previously found superiority of the "gifted" as regards to temperament stems much more from the socioeconomic level at which most gifted children are found than from other difference in "gifted" children as such. When socioeconomic background is taken into account relatively few significant differences are found between "gifted" and others. But when the parent background of these children is disregarded, there seems to be differences in seven of the ten areas measured and in all these areas the "gifted" child has superior temperament. [8]

Dauw tested 712 public high school seniors, who were the total population.

RESULTS

1. Significant chi squares were found on 35% of the items differentiating original thinkers from good elaborators and from those students highest in both abilities.

2. Previous research successfully identifying creative persons through biographical data was supported.[9]

In another report by Dauw testing life experiences of original thinkers and good elaborators, highly creative children were found to feel that their fathers strongly encourage them to be inventive. Highly creative boys felt their parents more interested in their achievements than low creative boys.

The highly creative tend to become so involved in projects that they don't take time out to eat or sleep. They also tend to set higher goals for themselves than they can reach.

Low creatives tend to have close friends almost always about their own age while the high creatives more often have friends almost always older.

High creatives tend to receive better marks than low creatives but the difference is not very great in high school. They also prefer a more competitive or independent work relationship with others while the whole question seems to make little difference to the low creatives. The highly creatives also make up games, build

models, compose music, play musical instruments, paint, participate in dramatics, and dabble more in woodworking and tinkering.

The highly creative girls like to attend lectures as often as
possible as do the boys.

There was no important differences between creativity levels in
attending athletic events, churches, dances and social parties.

Athletically the low creative students tended to participate
more often in track, golf, hockey, wrestling and gymnastics. Only
in tennis did the highly creative boys tend to participate more
often.

High creatives are recognized for school honors more often and
volunteered more answers in class. They had more leadership
positions in school organizations and seemed to view those
teachers as "best" who were strict. Intellectual matters seem to be
discussed more often between parents and their highly creative
students. They were often turned to by peers for advice. Low
creatives were more problems in discipline.[10]

ANXIETY

In the Feldhusen study, forty children were tested in the 7, 8, 9
grades which were divided equally into four groups; high-anxious
boys, high-anxious girls, low-anxious boys and low-anxious girls.
Self-rated tests indicated that students tend to rate themselves
higher in creativity than did their teachers. There was no significant differences between anxiety or sex groups in performance on
the battery of five divergent thinking tests. The low anxiety boys
however rated themselves as did their teachers as having the most
creative ability while the low-anxiety girls rated themselves the
lowest for creativity. The explanation was that the girls reacted to
societal expectations. Most significant finding was that society
rather than anxiety inhibits. [11]

READING PREFERENCES

Roderick's choice was 100 sixth graders in three schools in
central Pennsylvania that were enrolled in the Explorers' Book
Club. Scores on three verbal tasks of the Minnesota Tests of
Creative Thinking were available for each subject. Composite
scores ranged from 28 to 248. Scores on Lorge Thorndike
Intelligence Scale for this population ranged from 78 to 143.

The high and the middle creatives in this study liked and read more books than did the low creatives. Less creativity appears to be more of a detriment to reading than more creativity an asset.

The reading patterns of the low creatives in this investigation suggest that the onus for opening the doors of literature to this group be placed on the classroom teacher.

The greater appeal that reading had for the more creative child concurs with Selye's statement that some creative scientists can be classified as bookworms. Taylor's findings also support this conclusion.

Results of investigation suggest that children's preferences for types of literature generally appeared to be related to sex but not to creativity.

The one exception was biography. Biography was preferred by the high and middle creatives. The study suggests that preferences of children of varying degrees of creativity tended to agree with a panel of authorities' predictions of them. The high, middle, and low creatives differed significantly in the number of books they read from the total list and from those rated as appealing to most creative children.

Boys and girls differed significantly in preferences for fantasy, realistic fiction, biography and information but not poetry.

High, middle and low creatives did differ significantly in their preferences for books judged to appeal to the most creative child but not for those judged to appeal to the least creative.

Children commented more on factors relating to literary components and format of the books while the judges spoke more of character, reader involvement and external influences.

High creatives commented more frequently about reader involvement, literary components, and format than did the low creatives.[12]

SENSE OF HUMOR

Tarratus investigated relationships between creativity in music and sex, academic aptitude, grades, music skills and jazz experience. The results showed no significant correlation between any of the scores on the Creativity Battery and (1) a measure of scholastic aptitude, (2) tests of musical skills and information, (3) music theory grades, (4) total university grades, and (5) graduate grades. There were low correlations between various parts of the creativity battery and music notation speed, Freshman English grades, applied music grades and jazz experience. The males did slightly better on four creativity scores.

The humor test developed in this study was the most excellent discriminator of composers from other music students. Creative musicians possess a sense of humor and demonstrate a high incidence of humor in their total output. Both the humor test and the ratio scoring technique are superior tools for discriminating creative from less creative music students, producing high multiple correlations (R's) on the order of .60 which may be used in regression form for the prediction or selection of potential composers. [13]

If there is one general characteristic to be singled out which seems to appear repeatedly in researching the gifted-creative student, it is very definite sense of humor. Whether the humor is positive or negative depends on the circumstances, but one thing is certain, almost all gifted-creative students have a sense of humor. It is an excellent measure for creativity. We have found in our own research with these students, humor, more than any other characteristics is constantly brought to light.

After reading the material contained in this Chapter, the educator should be more comfortable in distinguishing the "gifted high I.Q." student or high performance student from the "gifted-creative."

The material should also be quite helpful if the teacher needs to prepare a report for the Superintendent or School Board regarding course structure for a gifted-creative student. By having the necessary material such as this accumulated conveniently, the music director should have been able to save many hours of library research time.

---

[1] Torrance, E. Paul, *"Scientific Views of Creativity & Factors Affecting its Growth,"* DAEDALUS, Vol. 94, No. 3, Summer, 1965.

[2] Cicirelli, Victor, *"Form of the Relationship Between Creativity, I.Q. and Academic Achievement,* JOURNAL OF EDUCATIONAL PSYCHOLOGY, Vol. 56, Dec. 1956, pp. 303-308.

[3] Edwards, Meredith and Tyler, Leona, *"Intelligence, Creativity and Achievement in a Non-selective Public Junior High School,"* JOURNAL OF EDUCATIONAL PSYCHOLOGY, Vol. 56 April 1965, No. 29, pp. 96-99.

[4] Skager, Rodney W. and Schultz, Charles B., Klein, Stephen P., *"Quality and Quantity of Accomplishments as Measures of Creativity,"* JOURNAL OF EDUCATIONAL PSYCHOLOGY, Vol. 56, Feb. 1956, pp. 31-39.

[5]Yamamoto, Kaoru, *"Creativity and Unpredictability in School Achievement,"* THE JOURNAL OF EDUCATIONAL RESEARCH, Vol. 60, No. 7, March 1967, pp. 331-335.

[6]Klausmeier, Herbert J. *"Cognitive Learning Outcomes II,"* JOURNAL OF EDUCATIONAL PSYCHOLOGY, 1961, pp. 210, 211.

[7]Wonderly, Donald M. and Fleming, Elyse S. *"Underachievement and the Intelligent Creative Child,"* JOURNAL OF THE INTERNATIONAL COUNCIL FOR EXCEPTIONAL CHILDREN, Vol. 31, Sept. 1964 to May 1966, pp. 405-409.

[8]Bonsall, Marcella R., and Steffire, Buford, "The Temperment of Gifted Children." CALIFORNIA JOURNAL OF EDUCATIONAL RESEARCH 1955, Vol. 6, pp. 162-165.

[9]Dauw, D.C., *"Life Experiences of Original Thinkers and Good Elaborators,"* EXCEPTIONAL CHILDREN, March 1966, pp. 433-440. Copyrighted by The Council for Exceptional Children, Reprinted by permission.

[10]Dauw, Dean C., *"Life Experiences of Original Thinkers and Good Elaborators,"* *(Part II)* EXCEPTIONAL CHILDREN, Vol. 32 September 1965-1966. Copyrighted by The Council for Exceptional Children, Reprinted by permission.

[11]Feldhusen, John F. and Denny, Terry, *"Teachers & Children Perceptions of Creativity in High and Low-Anxious Children,"* THE JOURNAL OF EDUCATIONAL RESEARCH, Vol. 58 July-Aug. 1965 No. 10 p. 442.

[12]Roderick, Jessie A. *"Some Relationships Between Creativity & the Reading Preferences and Choices of a Group of Sixth Graders,"* JOURNAL OF THE ASSOCIATION FOR SUPERVISION AND CURRICULUM DEVELOPMENT NEA EDUCATIONAL LEADERSHIP, October 1968.

[13]Tarratus, Edward Arthur Jr., *"Creative Processes in Music and the Identification of Creative Music Students,"* DISSERTATION ABSTRACTS, 1965 pp. 6679, 6680.

CHAPTER 2

Analyzation and Testing Students for Gifted Programs

Creativity tests are an important adjunct to achievement, performance and I.Q. tests when used as an aid in identifying the gifted student. E. Paul Torrance, Ph.D., (who is presently Chairman of the Department of Educational Psychology at the University of Georgia) has compiled the "Torrance Tests of Creative Thinking." This test comes in two forms, it is suggested that the Figural Form A be used in meeting the needs of music educators in determining which students are high or above average creatives.

The *Torrance Test of Creative Thinking (Figural A for all grades)* are booklets available in lots of twenty-five with scoring worksheets, manual, key, and record sheet. They will not send complimentary specimen sets and the purchaser must be identified by title and school or organization preferable on school stationery. Order by mailing your request to:

> Personnel Press, Inc.
> A Division of Ginn and Company
> 20 Nassau Street
> Princeton, New Jersey 08540

Prices are: 1-9 pkgs. $5.00, 10-39 pkgs. $4.75 pkg; 40 or more pkgs. $4.50.

Although it is not necessary to use the technical manual for grading purposes, it is suggested that a Norms-Technical Manual,

Research Edition at $1.00 a copy be available to the test administrator. This manual is an invaluable aid for background information regarding the tests and a storehouse of excellent quick reference material on Creativity should the need for pertinent information become necessary.

Time spent reading the technical manual before administering the test will equip the administrator with guided insight and will assist in answering definitively questions that may occur during testing.

TESTING PROCEDURE AND METHOD

It is advisable to test incoming freshmen vocal or instrumental students since they will primarily be the bulk of the group to be channeled into various gifted programs throughout the entire four academic years. A desirable approach would be to test most music students the same day using two teaching personnel rather than one. The test administrators can then check tests and cross check each other. By testing the same day, students cannot exchange thoughts and thereby cause less of a validity problem. Basically the morning class hours are preferable with Tuesday, Wednesday, Thursday as possible times. Avoid the fatigue days of Monday or Friday. If more than one testing day must be used, test the same hour each day in the morning. The months of November or March are good because this leaves most music teachers free from concerts, tours, football and basketball activities or term examinations. It also allows a reasonable amount of time for April or December vacation should additional time be necessary for correcting tests.

DO NOT announce in advance that students are to be tested the next day. Choose a class time to hand out tests as a pleasing break in routine. Motivation is the key to Creativity and this procedure is quite acceptable.

DIALOGUE FOR TESTING

Before testing it is well to prepare a prescribed dialogue and remain with it throughout. A workable dialogue follows:

"Class we are going to do a little something different today; measure your Creativity potential. This little pamphlet which will be passed out cannot be measured in pass or fail grades like achievement, I.Q. or performance tests. We want you to have a little fun with it. Let your imagination go as "wild" as it can. We know that many of you enjoy drawing figures around the border of your papers when you should be taking notes. Some of you just enjoy "doodling" on the wall or paper when talking on the phone. This is what we desire you to do with this pamphlet. Each illustration should suggest something to you. Draw that subject, anything, no matter how silly it may seem. After the completion of each drawing be certain to print the title describing the drawing. We aren't interested in how well you draw but in how many ideas you have drawn. If you are finished before time please sit quietly and do not disturb the remainder of the class. Do not turn the page until you are instructed to do so. Any questions?"

This type of dialogue along with a few jokes from the administering teacher should establish a relaxed atmosphere which is essential to creative testing. Should any questions arise during the test, instruct students to raise their hand and have someone go directly to that student's aid. Normally very few questions are asked but the teacher should become acquainted with the test and manual prior to administering the test.

GRADING CREATIVITY TESTS

After testing has been completed, it must be decided whether to send the pamphlets back to have them hand-scored or to score them yourself. Trained personnel whom Dr. Torrance has taught, do the hand-scoring. If the decision is to have trained personnel score the test, check the latest address on the pamphlet included within the Creativity test box.

Basic service which includes booklets scored, raw and T score entered on scoring worksheets and booklets returned cost $1.35 per booklet. If a class list is desired, a report in triplicate, listing students alphabetically giving pupil and class identification together with raw and T scores and medians, is available for an additional .15 per pupil. The distribution report in triplicate will be given with raw scores for all booklets with seven scores per pupil. Medians and quartiles will be indicated at .15 per pupil. The means and standard deviations are .05 per pupil extra. An IBM work card can be prepared giving pupil data, raw and derived scores at .10 per pupil. Press-on label with pupil date is .10 per student.

If funds are limited, the basic service is sufficient. However, the Torrance test can be scored by the test administrator but requires time and patience.

SELF-SCORING CREATIVITY TESTS

If the decision is to do all the test scoring by the test administrator then take the following steps:

Step 1:

Adhere religiously to the *Torrance Tests of Creative Thinking Directions Manual and Scoring Guide. DO NOT* deviate or insert your own subjectivity.

Step 2:

Leaf through the booklets and weed out those who have completed the illustrations most completely. Set these booklets to one side. When you have completed this procedure with the entire group of test booklets, take these well-elaborated booklets that have been set aside and rearrange them at RANDOM through the entire group again. Try to avoid placing two well-elaborated booklets together. This technique is especially helpful to the person doing the scoring as it avoids mental fatigue.

Step 3:

A problem that may be encountered is which elaboration on a high-creative test should be counted. Even the test booklet doesn't have all the answers. A helpful hint is to watch carefully for shading, changes in drawing patterns, small details and other miniature objects drawn around the major subject. It is easy to overlook a small elaboration.

Step 4:

If questions arise, it is well to check the manual. Another good procedure to follow is to have another teacher also grading these tests. Should a questionable booklet or booklets arise pass them on to the other teacher to re-grade lightly in pencil. Discuss your evaluation with this teacher. Between the two, a more objective evaluation grade should result.

Step 5:

When scoring use a red pen for *Elaboration* identification and a blue ballpoint for *Originality*. This makes totaling and analysis easier. Use the following codes:

Fluency-ff
Flexibility-f
Originality-O
Elaboration-E

For the total place the letter then grade ie., E-23, f-28, ff-31, O-38 Total -120. Place total scores above each printed title consistently in all booklets.

Step 6:

Avoid grading in mass. Don't get discouraged if you lose patience.

Put tests aside and try again a half hour later. Grading tests of this nature over a longer period of time rather than attempting to do all at once is most desirable.

Step 7:

Tabulate scores for fluency, flexibility, originality and elaboration and place the total in red on the upper right hand corner of the face of the booklet. This total will be easily accessible when charting.

PREPARING CHARTS FOR ANALYSIS

Prepare a Creativity Tabulation chart by listing the highest score on the top of the page and placing the lowest last. Divide the group in half obtaining a median score. Section the scores in groups of four; high creative, above average creative, average and below average creatives. This procedure allows the maximum number of students to be selected for a gifted program, rather than the selected few. Should you desire a highly accelerated curriculum program then select only the high creatives for consideration.

Most music educators have a special test to measure performance and accountability. The *Watkins-Farnum Performance*

Scale Form A is one such test with significant reliability scored at .95. In charting, the word Farnum applies to this test. Should future use of statistics be needed for correlating or standard deviation in further research a suggestion might be to take your raw score, whether it be on the Farnum test or a measurement of your choosing and convert the letter score with values as follows: A-50, B-40, C plus-30, C-20, D plus-10, and D-1. This value system allows more accurate ranking.

This method also allows computation for rank-difference correlation if use is to be made in comparing I.Q. to Creativity, Creativity to Performance, Performance to I.Q. or the combination of choice. The charts are established in this manner to allow maximum of future use and flexibility.

For performance charting obtain the median in performance and chart according to levels of achievement; high performers, above average performers, average performers, below average performers.

When testing students in a non-performance field such as Music Appreciation, Music History, Theory or Aesthetics courses, use the letter grade as you would for performance, converting to the value listed in performance as A-50, B-40 and so forth. Use the heading of the course on the chart in place of the Farnum Performance Tally. Take the grade after the first semester to obtain a more accurate evaluation.

From the accumulated administrative records obtain the students I.Q. score and tabulate those within the testing program with a rating ONLY of 110 or more.

To prepare a tally chart gather the cumulative record scores from I.Q., performance and creativity and parallel on a chart. This particular tabulation will be most useful in analyzation because the students rank on the chart will determine proper placement.

The chart has been extended to include a column for freshmen, sophomore, junior or senior placement because maturity does matter to educators in organizing curriculum. A general philosophy is to fit the program to the student rather than use maturity as a determining factor. It is recognized however that scheduling at times prohibits this philosophical use.

The Expectancy Grid and Scattergram are used primarily to determine precisely whether a group that is being tested may cluster around high performance, high creativity or vice versa. The charts serve as helpful indicators in scheduling particular groups of students into gifted classes. If a teacher is fortunate to have a large percentage of high-creatives entering in the freshman year, it is well to design gifted programs into the curriculum during the summer session or for the following school year. Any combination of two areas may be charted. Performance and Creativity, Performance and I.Q., or Creativity and I.Q. This placement does not mean to imply that we believe that performance and creativity are directly related. We use this merely as a sample chart for setting up a Scattergram or Expectancy Grid if the teacher is not familiar with this type of charting. Should a student reveal high scores in Performance and I.Q. you have a potential candidate for the Student Instructor program. Should a student be placed high in Creativity you just may have a potential composer. The proof of the programs remains with analysis and use by the teacher.

If a cluster of high-creative, high I.Q. students prevail, a highly accelerated gifted group will result. Curriculum for a two or three year program rather than two or three gifted programs in one year is suggested. The group of students will then receive a "block" of gifted enrichment rather than having to choose between the gifted programs in a particular year.

The temptation at this point is to become a bit discouraged with the amount of time that must be used to test and chart. A good way to eliminate some of this consuming task is to have a master teacher, mature secretary, your wife or husband do the charting of these students. All that is needed is the statistical breakdown of test scores in Creativity and Performance to work up the Scattergram, Expectancy Grid or Tally charts. Be certain to convert the raw performance scores to a letter grade because the number score on a music test does not coincide with the normal mental reference given to test evaluations. All charts are designed to be simple and do not require a complexity of knowledge. DO NOT use a student assistant for this task however, due to the confidential nature of the information.

After charts have been completed, place in a loose leaf folder covering each chart with plastic. These charts will be referred to continually through the year of administrating the gifted program and this type of treatment is most essential.

CHART ANALYZATION

For specific analyzation of charts a good procedure to follow is to scan the brief explanations listed below.

STATISTICAL RANK BREAKDOWN is an accumulation of test scores in Creativity, Performance and I.Q. beginning with the highest score and ranked to the lowest. Symbols are used in each category to determine precisely what the student can qualify for in a gifted program. Three symbols beside the name denotes a highly accelerated student with fine potential in all programs. Different symbols indicate which program a student belongs in. The symbol # + designates a gifted performer, the symbol * + a gifted creative. When only one symbol is given, this student may do well initially in one program. A student with only this symbol (*) means that all programs with creative structure would best fit this student. Because the symbol (+) or gifted is missing, one cannot expect as great an amount of acceleration as the student with a three-symbol classification. The student with the symbol (#) may only perform well on an instrument or voice because of years of training and it would be well to keep such a student again only in the performance program if maximum acceleration is desired. To maintain a proper amount of gifted acceleration, only students with above and high ranking scores qualify for the symbols.

TALLY OF FARNUM, TORRANCE AND I.Q. SCORES is a chart designed to give the instructor an immediate summation of test scores and year for each student. It is a necessary and essential chart for explaining the reasons why each student has been chosen for the gifted program.

EXPECTANCY GRID is used primarily to determine what tested students, as a group, reveal. Thirty students tested in this analysis show only thirteen above or higher in performance. Creativity as a group ranks even with fifteen above and higher and fifteen below. As a group a music educator can plan for a program of thirteen gifted performers and fifteen gifted creatives.

SCATTERGRAM is helpful in determining a pattern or trend a particular group tends to follow. A clustering of stars would show a definite predictable pattern. On this particular chart no trend emerges since the stars are fairly well scattered. If a cluster of stars appeared in the 40 or 50 column around the 124 and above Creativity scores, this would be indicative of a highly creative, gifted group of students with a potential of great expectations. If only one star is revealed, it would do the music teacher well to determine which student that represents and begin developing this talent.

RANK-DIFFERENCE CORRELATION is a statistical chart mainly used to determine if there is a parallel between Creativity and Performance or any other area one wishes to compare. From this chart one can derive the mathematics necessary for establishing a statistical formula for standard deviation. Normally most music educators need not go this far in statistics but as program justification may be called upon, this chart is essential.

INDIVIDUAL ANALYZATION OF A GIFTED STUDENT

To extend clarification in choosing a gifted student, let us take Dawn J. and follow her progress on the charts. On the creativity test she ranked 146, second from the top of thirty students which is a high-creative. Her I.Q. is 120. In performance she is a (B) student but ranks thirteenth in the music score. This student is a good candidate for both the gifted and the gifted-creative programs and should definitely be included in future gifted curriculum programs. Her acceleration in the gifted program will also depend on getting her performance record beyond the thirteenth rank, although this is quite good when compared to other students.

Todd J. however ranks last on the creativity test when measured with thirty students in this same group. His performance is (A) with a ranking of 3. His I.Q. is 125. This student's acceleration would be very poor if directed into creative writing of half-time shows since this program is designed for the high-creative. Todd would accelerate well in the Student Instructor program if his personality meets his high performance rating. This is the section where subjectivity does enter. It will be the teacher's choice whether Todd should teach other students. Should Todd have a timid personality and not desire the Student-Teacher program then the teacher would direct him into the Comparative-Arts program which should challenge his high I.Q. or the Guitar class which should challenge his high performance proficiency and extend this proficiency to another instrument.

INDIVIDUAL ANALYZATION FOR
PSYCHOLOGICAL UNDERSTANDING

It seems almost an impossibility that a busy music teacher with an oversupply of students is often the best counselor. Unlike other forms of instruction, the music student often continues with music in all four years of his schooling and the music teacher gets to know students well. Extra rehearsals and the personal contact made during tours, concerts and extra-curricular performances also intensifies this relationship. A busy music educator can be an excellent counselor with a little assistance from a test and the desire to help students.

Charts, symbols or identifiable research are only tools to help an educator individually analyze a particular student. It is well to think of the programs designed for an "individual" and not as a group since this is the primary objective. Identification is the key and individual understanding the incentive. Before folding away the charts or stocking the Creativity tests, re-open the file and again review the booklets of those students who rank above and high on the tests. Do they reveal a psychological trend, such as sense of humor, symbols of being lost, negative designs encompassing symbols of destruction? Understanding is complex and the number of music students within a program often prohibits such needed insight. An excellent source of information beyond I.Q. and performance is the revelations made by the *Torrance Test of Creativity.* Since it is based on a psychological structure.

To further explain this procedure let us take Jayne G. with a Creativity score of 147. In most gifted programs this student would have been eliminated since her I.Q. is 111 and her performance is C+. Normally she was a B student in other academic subjects and quite a pleasant person. One of her parents was blind and the girl seemed to have adjusted quite well to the family handicap. It came as a surprise after analyzing the Creativity test that all of Jayne's symbols were negative—reflecting knives, monsters and other symbols of destruction. Even though test responses were negative, they were highly imaginative and quite elaborate and Jayne came out as one of our most creative students. After a few personal interviews the truth surfaced that Jayne wasn't as well adjusted and positive as her teachers had believed. Insight such as this helped to develop Jayne's positive creativity and proper counseling assisted in better family adjustment. Without this testing analysis and interest a highly creative student might have slipped past for another year in her academic career.

Less dramatic but equally effective was the case of Dennis K. He was a high creative-gifted student but doing poorly in performance on his instrument. His grades in school never went above a C even though his I.Q. suggested better things. His delightful sense of humor and carefree attitude would not lead one to suspect that he missed his father's companionship dramatically. Originally the father held a key position in a business run from the home. Dennis was comfortable having father around for years but in his late teens father changed the business in a more commercial sense outside the home. Dennis saw his father little. As a rebellion, he chose to get lower grades as *"payment"* for a father that chose business over children. This was information procured from extensive interviews. The Creativity test was reviewed and two interesting pictures revealed the underlying factor of Dennis and his problem. One picture displayed a lady bug looking for its child. In the other picture it showed a baby bug lost and looking for its mother. The music director suggested to the parents that a desk be placed in father's new place of business for Dennis to do his homework. The results in improved grades and more devoted practice on his musical instrument resulted in a complete turnover of previous carefree, undisciplined behavior.

It doesn't take a lot of time to review these tests and sometime insights can result in dramatic correction and guidance. The music director can be an excellent counselor.

There is but one basic rule to follow when teaching a program for the gifted—STEP ASIDE AND GUIDE. It is natural to follow a pattern of directing any educational curriculum from the front of class in a somewhat lecture form. This procedure does not work well with gifted students because talent and "giftedness" often run a music teacher to near exhaustion with academic demands. Each program is therefore built with the safeguard design of individualized instruction encompassing extra credit, independent study, enrichment, or individualized progress curriculum. Acceleration therefore is threefold. The first means is to fit the student to the

STATISTICAL RANK BREAKDOWN OF TEST SCORES

	Creativity *		Performance #		IQ +
H	147	Jayne G *	A	Jodell G. *#+	135	Kim C. +#
I	146	Dawn J. *#+	A	Phil H. *#+	130	Gregg G. *+
G	139	Jackie G. *+	A	J. Jean W. *#+	129	Phil H. *#+
H	134	Dennis K. *+	A	Chelle C. #	124	Dennis K. *+
	124	Gregg G. *+	A	Kim C. #+	124	Allison C. +
	112	Doug W. *#	A	Roger J. #+	122	Roger J. #+
	111	Janice G. *	A	Karen K. #+	121	Todd J. #+
			A	Todd J. #+	120	Dawn J. #+
A	109	Dick G. *				
B	109	Jodell G. *#+	B	Dawn J. *#+	119	Karen K. #+
O	101	Craig C. *	B	Kevin J. #	117	Kris K. +
V	101	Robert G. *	B	Doug. W. #*	116	Jodell G. #+
E	100	Wendy W. *+	B	Tracy W. #	116	Wendy K. *+
	100	Walter K. *	B	Kathy K. #	115	Jackie G. *+
	95	J. Jean W. *#+			115	J. Jean W. *#+
	92	Phil H. *#+	C+	Jayne G.		
			C+	Janice G.	113	Tracy W.
	87	Tracy W.	C+	Wendy W.	112	Janice G.
A	87	Kevin J.	C+	Allison C.	112	Walter K.
V	86	Allison C.	C+	Gary G.	111	Gary G.
E	86	Chelle C.	C+	Camille K.	111	Chelle C.
R	85	Robbie G.	C	Jackie G.	111	Jayne G.
A	84	Kim C.	C	Gregg G.	110	Signe K.
G	82	Gary G.	C	Craig C.	108	Kathy K.
E	82	Signe K.	C	Robbie G.	108	Dick G.
			C	Signe K.	107	David K.
	81	Roger J.			107	Craig C.
	71	Camille K.	D+	Dick G.	106	Robbie G.
	70	Kathy K.	D+	Robert G.	105	Robert G.
L	64	David K.	D+	Kris K.		
O	61	Karen K.	D	Dennis K.	99	Doug. W.
W	58	Kris K.	D	Walter K.	98	Kevin J.
	55	Todd J.	D	David K.	93	Camille K.

program through proper identification. A second part of acceleration is to use programs around the standard classroom so that the student chooses material according to interest and talent and gives according to ability. The third form is dependent on the amount

TALLY OF FARNUM, TORRANCE AND I.Q. SCORES

Name	Year	Farnum Raw	Farnum Converted	Farnum Letter	Torrance Total	IQ
Jayne G.	S	15	30	C+	147	111
Dawn J.	F	20	40	B	146	120
Jackie G.	Sr.	10	20	C	139	115
Dennis K.	Sr.	1	1	D	134	124
Gregg G.	F	10	20	C	124	130
Doug W.	F	20	40	B	112	99
Janice G.	Sr.	15	30	C+	111	112
Dick G.	Sr.	5	10	D+	109	108
Jodell G.	F	25	50	A	109	116
Craig C.	F	15	20	C	101	107
Robert G.	F	5	10	D+	101	105
Wendy W.	S	15	30	C+	100	116
Walter K.	Sr.	1	1	D	100	112
J. Jean W.	F	25	50	A	95	115
Phil H.	F	25	50	A	92	129
Tracy W.	F	20	40	B	87	113
Kevin J.	S	20	40	B	87	98
Allison C.	F	15	30	C+	86	124
Chelle C.	F	25	50	A	86	111
Robbie G.	F	10	20	C	85	106
Kim C.	S	25	50	A	84	135
Gary G.	S	15	30	C+	82	111
Signe K.	Sr.	10	20	C	82	110
Roger J.	F	25	50	A	81	122
Camille K.	Sr.	15	30	C+	71	93
Kathy K.	Sr.	20	40	B	70	108
David K.	Jr.	1	1	D	64	107
Karen K.	Sr.	25	50	A	61	119
Kris K.	Jr.	5	10	D+	58	117
Todd J.	F	25	50	A	55	121

Farnum Mean Score 29.1
Torrance Mean   95.3
Codes: F-Freshman, S-Sophomore, Jr.-Junior, Sr.-Senior

of time the teacher will spend on structuring the material suggested to be used as guidelines. Greater input results in better acceleration.

EXPECTANCY GRID

Torrance Test Scores on Creativity	Watkin's-Farnum Test Scores				TOTAL
	Below Average 1 to 10	Average Performers 20 to 30	Above Average Performers 40	High Performers 50	
High Creatives 111 and above	1	1111	11		7
Above Average Creatives 92 to 110	111	11		111	8
Average Creatives 82-91		1111	11	11	8
Low Creatives 55 to 81	11	1	1	111	7
TOTALS	6	11	5	8	30

Grid shows how scores on Creativity test and Watkins-Farnum Music Test are tallied in cells.

SCATTERGRAM

Creativity
Scores   *Farnum Scores*

Creativity Scores	1	10	20	30	40	'50
147				*		
146					*	
139			*			
134	*					
124			*			
112					*	
111			*	*		
109		*				*
101			*	*		
100	*			*		
95						*
92						*
87					**	
86				*		*
85						
84						*
82			*	*		
81						*
71				*		
70					*	
64	*					
61						*
58		*				
55						*
TOTALS	3	2	5	7	5	8

RANK-DIFFERENCE CORRELATION

Name of Student	Creative Rank	Farnum Score *	Creative Rank	Music Rank	Diff. in Rank Scores	Diff. in Rank Sq'd Scores
Jayne G.	147	28(30)	1	19	-18	324
Dawn J.	146	20(40)	2	13	-11	121
Jackie G.	139	10(20)	3	21	-18	324
Dennis K.	134	1(1)	4	30	-26	676
Gregg G.	124	10(20)	5	22	-17	289
Doug W.	112	20(40)	6	10	- 4	16
Janice G.	111	15(30)	7	15	- 8	64
Jodell G.	109	25(10)	8	2	6	36
Richard G.	109	5(10)	9	26	-17	289
Craig C.	101	15(20)	10	24	-14	196
Robert G.	101	5(10)	11	25	-14	196
Wendy W.	100	15(30)	12	18	- 6	36
Walter K.	100	1(1)	13	29	-16	256
J. Jean W.	95	25(50)	14	6	8	64
Philip H.	92	25(50)	15	7	8	64
Tracy W.	87	20(40)	16	11	5	25
Kevin J.	87	20(40)	17	9	8	64
Allison C.	86	25(50)	18	5	13	169
Chelle C.	86	15(30)	19	14	5	25
Robbie G.	85	10(20)	20	23	- 3	9
Kim C.	84	25(50)	21	8	13	169
Gary G.	82	15(30)	22	17	5	25
Signe K.	82	10(20)	23	20	3	9
Roger J.	81	25(50)	24	1	23	329
Camille K.	71	15(30)	25	16	9	81
Kathy K.	70	20(40)	26	12	14	196
David K.	64	1(1)	27	28	- 1	1
Karen K.	61	25(50)	28	4	24	576
Kris K.	58	5(10)	29	27	2	4
Todd J.	55	25(50)	30	3	27	729
					TOTAL	5,462

*Star over column designated transposed Farnum scores from raw total to letter than to values: A-20, B-40, C+-30, C-20, D+-10, D-1.

A busy music educator has very little time for complicated set-ups or for extending present curriculum, therefore it is suggested that music lists, maps, charts and bibliographies be held to a minimum to avoid duplicating material a teacher may already have accumulated. Any material suggested is presented with a minimum music budget in mind. If a lengthy list appears it is to be used as quick reference material when or during future supplies which are not an absolute MUST to operate the programs. Often, with imagination, books, films, and records can be substituted from the school's present library and A.V. materials.

Part 2

INDIVIDUALIZED PROGRAMS
FOR DEVELOPING
GIFTED MUSIC STUDENTS

CHAPTER 3

Training Gifted Music Students
to Write Half-Time Shows

Most band directors appreciate interesting half-time shows with contemporary ideas. An excellent source of talent is the gifted student because it is this type of student that possesses a great amount of divergent thinking. Half-time shows require just this ingredient to make for a successful presentation. The challenge of performance adds immediate interest for the gifted and results visually draw a great deal of satisfaction.

This particular curriculum is set up independently of the instructor. The music director is an answering agent and editor. When speaking of half-time shows we do not mean the complete product with complicated drills and mechanical placement of instruments. What is basically desired are new workable ideas which can be performed.

What better way to stimulate the creative thought process than to promise a performance of a particular "brain child" before the student body and perhaps an audience of 1,000 or 2,000 people. This isn't as far-fetched as it may seem if just a little planning is involved.

SCHEDULING

Since the overcrowded school day does not permit extra minutes for many beneficial activities regarding the gifted, a workable schedule can be achieved first by checking your own schedule. Most band directors have jazz band rehearsals, band parents' meeting, band board meetings, check-in time before and after school, or if they are lucky, a period of preparation. Normally the gifted creative student is very easy to supervise. It is therefore quite easy to make available a practice room, band room or any other area which would most comfortably achieve the purpose of laying out research work necessary for developing a half-time show. Type two lists of scheduled times for that month and place them on the bulletin board in the music room and the portable bookrack which will contain all the necessary resource books.

The schedule should read:

TIME SCHEDULE FOR CREATIVE WRITING PROJECT
HALF-TIME SHOWS

1. Before school   7:50 to 8:30 A.M.
2. Eighth period   3:40 to 4:30 P.M.
3. Thursday evenings   4:30 to 5:30 P.M.
4. After basketball games   8:00 to 9:00 P.M.

As long as the teacher must be in the building supervising other activities, there is no reason why students can't benefit from this time working on a project. Most students, however, favor spending the majority of time writing at home.

MATERIALS

Procure a moveable bookcase for the music department. Place all necessary books for this project on this cart. This portability will prove highly advantageous when moving from room to room due to overcrowded facilities. Books must not be checked out from the cart as too much time is consumed keeping track of missing materials. With books on the cart at all times, any student who wishes to do so can scan at any time. Many ideas were prompted in just this manner. Materials necessary for this project are:

1. Moveable bookcase
2. Books from the suggested booklist
3. Cassette tape recorder

4. Tapes or list of favorite fanfares
5. Library list of march music
6. Half-time supply catalogues
7. Yellow pages telephone book
8. Magna board
9. Minimum of 100 red magna men
10. Large chart sheet for magna board
11. Time schedule
12. Handout sheets of half-time requirements
13. Long table and two chairs
14. Charting ditto paper

When materials are thus gathered sufficiently to begin the program, the class must then be instructed on their use. Designate a particular place where the magna board, magna men, and bookcase will permanently be set. Usually a practice room off the main band or choir room is most desirable. Place all materials listed on the moveable bookcase with the exception of the magna board, magna-men and the half-time handout sheet requirement. These items are too easily damaged or lost. Keep these in your office. DO NOT mount the magna board but lay it on a long table. Students must put an eye just over the rim to get the proper perspective of the formation as seen from the stands. DO NOT allow more than two students working on a show together because this encourages socialization rather than industriousness. Far less problems evolve if two boys or two girls work together rather than couples. Encourage independent work habits with a show for each participating student. Even when shows sometime prove unworkable, learning experiences that are developed prove quite valuable. Perhaps too, one idea can be worked up from even a less desirable show.

PSYCHOLOGICAL ENCOURAGEMENT

To encourage students to write half-time shows, the divergent thinking process must be stimulated. Prior to beginning the program, take time in the classroom to discuss the half-time shows done that particular season for all your band students. Discuss the pros and cons of the show and ask how they think it might have been improved. If at all possible have the A.V. department video tape the shows so that the students can see and hear how they performed. This alone is quite surprising because many cannot hear the band as a group but only themselves and players in the immediate area.

During football season from September through January, stimulate discussion about what students have seen on television and what good ideas that may have been gleaned from this observation. Encourage students to take in half-time activities from surrounding schools either college or high school. Discuss parades and what groups appeared most favorably in them. Have the students think of these shows in three ways, musically, visually, with precision and improvement.

During half-time practice, ask students to suggest how a show can be improved. Have a few students sit in the stands and observe. Is there enough color on the field? What would be a better way to hear the woodwinds? What is an alternative to inclement weather? These are only a few ideas suggested for use as a "brainstorming" technique in developing a thrust for new ideas. If the students feel they are part of the creation of a show and not just participants, better shows will evolve and a psychological thought process will begin for the gifted-creatives in the group.

This technique may be continued outside the classroom. Some of the worst football shows have been saved by color on the field. Try to visualize a stage setting that was especially appealing in the theater, opera, play or T.V. and movies. What color combinations were particularily attractive? One girl excitedly entered class one morning and told of the lovely lavender dress tied with a turquoise sash that was so exciting on the stage. Who but an art teacher would think of placing turquoise with lavender? Students must keep in mind that the color combination must compliment the uniforms, overlay and the large green of the field. One student chose white as a prop only to find it merged with the white overlays. Awareness is the first step towards psychologically setting a student for developing good half-time shows.

BOOKLIST

Most band directors have a list of favorite books that they have been using for years in preparation of football half-time shows. Many listed no doubt have already been in the library. It would be advisable to compare this list. The suggested book list has been selected to cover pageantry, drill, patterns, a story, reflective music and dancing. This should offer the measure of flexibility in beginning ideas that is needed in helping to develop an interesting show.

For the director who may not have some of these books and desires to develop the absolute minimum of financial commitment for the beginning of such a program, use only the books with an asterisk. If the school board, band parents or administration have no desire to contribute until the program has been developed and proven, order only these books whose total would be under 60 dollars. If the director purchases these books from his own money, keep in mind that these are educational materials necessary for work and are tax deductible along with any other supplies incurred in developing this curriculum.

Those marked on the list with a plus sign are not books but pamphlets which have proved helpful. There are both pamphlets and books that will add flash to the overall effect of half-time shows. THE DRUM MAJOR'S MANUAL and AMERICAN DRUMMER were suggested by gifted students. If a particular drum major is not up to par, this well-illustrated pamphlet will help the gifted student become aware of the techniques needed for improvement.

The drummer pamphlet is an improved pocket edition of short street beats for drummers with solos, military street beats and assists in filling in the segue between transition selections from one formation or drill to another at a half-time show. It also includes fife, drum and bugle corps numbers. It should prove to be a real find. Directors should compile a booklist similar to the following for student reference.

BOOKLIST FOR HALF-TIME SHOW PREPARATION

*A MANUAL OF CLOSE ORDER DRILL by A.R. Casavant, 1955, A.R. Casavant, Chattanooga, Tennessee +

*AMERICAN DRUMMER by Edward B. Straight's, tenth edition, Frank's Drum Shop, Inc. 226 S. Wabash Ave., Chicago, Illinois +

BAND PAGEANTRY by Dr. William Patrick Foster, Hal Leonard Music, Inc. 1968, 64 East Second St. Winona, Minnesota

*FIELD ENTRANCES by A.R. Casavant, 1959, Southern Music

*MARCHING BAND MANEUVERS by Richard Lee Schilling, The Instrumentalist Co. 1418 Lake St. Evanston, Illinois +

*MARCHING AND DANCING BANDSMEN by Orin Dykae Ford, Ludwig Music Publishing Co. Cleveland, Ohio 1956 +

*MODERN MARCHING BAND TECHNIQUES by Jack Lee, Hal Leonard Music, 64 E. Second St., Winona, Minnesota

*NEW DIRECTIONS FOR MARCHING BANDS by William J. Moody, Robbins Music Corporation, New York, N.Y. 1970 BIG 3 +

PATTERNS OF MOTION, Master Planning Guide Book 1 Concepts and Basic Patterns by Wm. C. Moffit, Hal Leonard Music Inc. 64 E. 2nd St.

PATTERNS OF MOTION, Master Planning Guide Book 2 by William C. Moffit, Hal Leonard Music Inc. 64 E. 2nd St. Winona, Minn.

PATTERNS OF MOTION, 96 Piece Band, Staging Designs and Conversions, by Wm. C. Moffit, Hal Leonard Music Inc. 64 E. 2nd St. Winona, Minn.

PRECISION DRILL by A.R. Casavant, 1957, Southern Music Co. 1100 Broadway, San Antonio 6, Texas

PRECISION DRILL LINE MOVEMENT, 1958, Southern Music Co.

PRECISION FLASH, A.R. Casavant, 1961, Southern Music Co.

STREET PARADE DRILLS by A.R. Casavant, 1959, Southern Music Co.

THE DRUM MAJOR'S MANUAL by Richard L. Schory and Wm. F. Ludwig, Jr., Ludwig Drum Co., 1728 N. Damen Ave. Chicago, Illinois 60647 +

*THE FAST BREAK by A.R. Casavant, Southern Music Company, 1100 Broadway, San Antonio 6, Texas

THE MARCHING BAND by Charles L. Spohn and Richard W. Heine, Allyn and Bacon, Inc. Boston, Massachusetts.

*THE SHOW BAND by Al G. Wright, The Instrumentalist Co. Evanston, Illinois, 1957

THE HIGH SCHOOL MARCHING BAND by W.T. Binion, Jr., Parker Publishing Co. Englewood Cliffs, N.J., 1973

MUSIC LIST

Equal in necessity to the booklist is a summation list of all marching band music presently in the school musical library. If a list is not available, appoint a student to type this list of march music from the library index cards. When this accumulation has been completed, check carefully and keep on the list ONLY the arrangements which suitably maintain the maximum amount of musicality upon the vastness of the football field. Good football shows are hinged on the excellence of musical performance and even the most adept organization falls prey to poor arrangements or improper scoring.

Add to the present library list new music secured from reviewing scores at a music store or sample records. Some directors prefer ordering from a marching music catalog published by the various publishing companies and sent to directors. Unless the director's confidence in the composers and arrangers' ability, and there are some that are fairly consistent, this can be a treacherous procedure. If time prohibits adding new music during the coordinating of this program, use the catalogues as step-off points for music suggestions. Often the catalogue gives the newest contemporary arrangements of popular music which students like to use in compiling shows. Carefully check through these catalogues circling with a red felt pen the possibilities of a new music order so that the students avoid compiling a fine show around poor music.

Although there are many sources of marching band music catalogues, there are times when the director is not on a specific mailing list or is new to the school. A half dozen companies may send catalogues if the request is made on school letter-head stationery and signed by the director.

Cimino Publications Incorporated
436 Maple Avenue
Westbury, L.I. N.Y. 11590

Hal Leonard Music
Pointer Publications, Inc.
64 E. 2nd St.
Winona, Minnesota 55987

Musart Music Co. Inc.
731-35 Halsted St.
Chicago Heights, Illinois 60411

G. Schirmer Inc.
609 Fifth Ave.
N.Y., N.Y. 10017

Tempo Music Publications Inc.
P.O. Box 129
Chicago, Illinois

Woodbury Music Corporation
P.O. Box 448 Main St.
Woodbury, Connecticut 06798

If the music program is fairly new and the music library is not extensive, three excellent sources of possible music lists are:

1. THE INSTRUMENTALIST, Twenty-fifth Anniversary Issue, Vol. 25, No. 1 August 1970, pages 49-58

2. BUILDING A SUPERIOR SCHOOL BAND LIBRARY by Lawrence Intravaia, 1972, Parker Publishing, West Nyack, N.Y. 10994

3. BAND MUSIC GUIDE by The Instrumentalist Co., Evanston, Illinois

Along with the catalogues, music lists and copies of old football shows, occasionally university or college instructors in charge of marching courses are happy to share old ditto sheets or copies of shows students have compiled. All these are excellent sources of stimulation for students to use as reference. Additional music lists can also be obtained in this way. Most directors are cooperative in suggesting new arrangements and music which they find especially appealing. Take notes and add these suggestions to the music list.

Naturally the director's personal preferences always take priority. The final music list should contain these preferences, new music and a list of good arrangements agreed to by many directors. When the list is completed, duration of the selection should be written alongside the title.

DURATION

It would be very fortunate indeed if all music publishers would place the estimated time of the musical selections on march music, but until this day occurs it will save hours of editing on the director's part if duration is placed on all music. Appoint a student teacher or gifted student to put this information below each title of the march music on the library box cover containing the music. To assist in this job, the handy formula and chart listed below saves valuable hours in determining accurate duration:

$$x \text{ (in seconds)} = \frac{\text{Total number of beats x 60 sec.}}{\text{Cadence (beats per 60 sec.)}}$$

Example: $x = \dfrac{64 \times 60}{160}$ thus $x = 24$ sec.

See Table, p. 57.

It is amazing how much planning time is saved in arranging future programs when this task is accomplished. It also helps the students secure a show within the 12 minutes allotted the band for half-time performance. There are very few directors around who haven't been plagued by overtime on the field or a show too short in duration leaving the audience in an anticlimatic mood. A good show takes up the necessary seconds but isn't so long that the athletes run through the band to start the game. It serves students in preparing shows to remember: YOU ARE HONORED GUESTS AT AN ATHLETIC PERFORMANCE, ACT AND PLAN ACCORDINGLY.

TABLE

Cadence or M.M.	Marching Time-Table No. of Beats								Seconds!	
60	4	8	16	24	32	36	40	48	64	68	72
70	3.3	6.7	13.3	20	26.7	30	33.3	40	53.2	56.7	60
80	3	6	12	18	24	27	30	36	48	51	54
92	2.6	5.2	10.5	15.7	20.9	23.5	26	31.2	41.8	44.4	47
100	2.4	4.8	9.6	14.4	19.2	21.6	24	28.8	38.4	40.8	43.2
112	2.1	4.2	8.6	12.9	17.1	19.2	21.3	25.5	34.2	36.3	38.4
120	2	4	8	12	16	18	20	24	32	34	36
132	1.8	3.6	7.3	11	14.6	16.4	18.2	21.8	29.2	31	32.8
144	1.7	3.3	6.7	10	13.3	15	16.7	20	26.7	28	30
152	1.6	3.2	6.3	9.5	12.6	14.2	15.8	19	25.2	26.8	28.4
160	1.5	3	6	9	12	13.5	15	18	24	25.5	27
168	1.4	2.8	5.7	8.5	11.4	12.8	14.2	17	22.8	24.2	25.6
180	1.3	2.7	5.3	8	10.7	12	13.3	16	21.3	22.7	24
192	1.2	2.5	5	7.5	10	11.2	12.5	15	20	21.2	22.5
210	1.2	2.4	4.6	6.9	9.2	10.4	11.6	14	18.4	19.6	20.8
222	1.1	2.2	4.4	6.5	8.7	9.8	10.9	13.1	17.4	18.5	19.6
240	1	2	4	6	8	9	10	12	16	17	18

Table Prepared by
Band Director Lester C. Echart
Rittman, Ohio High School

HALF-TIME FLASH

The truly lasting memory of an interesting football show is usually the flash. This is the segment that most of your audience will understand and will set the reputation of the show. To stimulate the creative ideas of gifted-creative students in this direction, obtain a classified telephone directory of the largest city near you. Check the subheadings in the yellow pages for: FIRE-WORKS, COSTUMES-MASQUERADE & THEATRICAL, FLAGS AND BANNERS, FLOATS-PARADE, FLOODLIGHTS AND SEARCHLIGHTS. If the pages seem limited in a particular area go to the largest library nearest you for a more extensive list from another state.

For quick reference, items such as pom poms, pennants, buttons, cowbells, printed balloons and other materials use: ABC HALFTIME SUPPLY COMPANY, Box 867, Winona, Minnesota 55987. If you are looking for dramatic costumes for dance groups, sequin derby hats or other theatrical materials which work well for field effects check LEO'S ADVANCE THEATRICAL COMPANY, 125 North Wabash, Chicago, Illinois, 60602. Keep in mind that LEO will not make up just one costume and that the catalogue is printed in color and has proven a wonderful source of stimulating creative ideas for pageantry.

International flags as low as $7.00, state flags, banners, flag pole and accessories can be obtained quite inexpensively at: CHICAGO FLAG COMPANY, 823 South Wabash Avenue, Chicago, Illinois, 60605. Keep in mind that these catalogues may only be obtained upon request on the school letterhead with director's signature.

OTHER SUPPLIES

Although Magno-Men come in four colors so that the director can designate certain colors to certain squads, only one color is necessary for gifted student use. Magno-men in red run $14.50 for 100. It isn't necessary to order more than 100 because shows run beyond this number get too complicated for the gifted student to handle. The Magno-board is $9.50 and 25 large 23" by 35" grid charts are sufficient to use as background sheets for charting the formations. Order this equipment from: THE INSTRUMENTA-LIST CO., 1418 Lake St., Evanston, Ill. 60204.

Order a table 3 by 5 feet with two chairs. The board should be laid on the table and students work with this. Do not hang this board because students must check patterns at eye level. Most secondary school bleachers, unlike the university where patterns look quite effective, are quite low and often formations must be changed to accommodate this significant difference.

Figure 1

**Gifted students using Magna Board while
setting up for half-time show preparation**

The grid lines on a ditto sheet help to facilitate accurate formations. A director may make his own master ditto of the field and run off necessary copies for the students or may wish to purchase the ditto.

TAPE RECORDER

A small tape recorder and a library of tapes containing various fanfares are absolutely essential for dramatic entrances to a football show. Most directors have their particular theme fanfare, but variance always adds a spark of interest. Normally gifted students cannot read a fanfare score so must rely on their ear. Few like to take the time to have a band perform various fanfares, so a positive alternate is to have brass perform various fanfares as a section. Give the name and the number of the fanfare for easy identification on the tapes. A gifted-creative student then can use the fanfare most in context to the particular show that is to be performed. A Spanish show theme leads well to a bullfighter's entrance fanfare. It gives the audience a key to what is to come besides being an attention getter.

HALF-TIME SHOW GUIDELINES

Before a student can accurately establish necessary goals for procuring a set of ideas for a half-time show, there are a series of logistics a director must procure on the worksheet such as:

1. Number of band members required in the show
2. Location of the press box
3. Side that the football players will enter the field
4. Location of the visitors' stands
5. Amount budgeted for supplies, props, flags
6. Time limit of the show
7. Standard procedure for presenting the flag and National Anthem
8. Summation of any area the director chooses to avoid as themes; political, religious, ethnic, drugs or alcohol.

Just informing a gifted student he may not use a political theme this particular year is not enough, a student will demand more of an explanation. Recently a very creative show was written by a gifted-creative girl. The theme centered around the complexities of opening a new school. Since the situation was quite contemporary and the show cleverly presented and filled with humor, it was one of the best. However, the student was not aware of the behind-the-scenes negotiations with trade unions and some irate parents who were objecting to the long delay of the building's completion. WHEN THE DIRECTOR HAS A QUESTION AS TO APPLICABILITY OF A SHOW, IT IS BEST TO SUBMIT IT FOR APPROVAL OF THE PRINCIPAL. In this particular situation the show was merely edited by the director using a grand tour of the new building instead of the reasons for non-completion. Most of the humor was gone but the colorful props and excellent selection of music sustained the quality of the original show. The gifted-creative, although disappointed, still felt proud of the creation.

STUDENT WORKSHEET FOR HALF-TIME SHOW PREPARATION

Ditto copies of half-time worksheets serve as necessary guidelines for the student. Directors of the program may choose to add their own suggestions to the worksheet. For expediency sake, only twelve major points are outlined.

STUDENT HALF-TIME SHOW WORKSHEET

1. *Pick an original theme for the show*
   a. Be original but keep in mind students and parents in the stands.
   b. Consider happy themes even though seeming juvenile. Most people enjoy fantasy regardless of age.
   c. Review books in half-time library for possible ideas.
   d. Try to recall interesting ideas seen at movies, T.V. games, Variety shows, plays, Ice Capades, Musicals, Parades or Conventions.

2. *Choose music to fit the theme*
   a. Use band library list for suggestions.
   b. Review new music catalogues.
   c. Use selections you have enjoyed performing.
   d. Check Band Director's Guide, or any bibliography of field music.
   e. A handy source is music magazines with half-time march lists.
   f. Accumulate at least five musical selections totaling a maximum of ten minutes total.

3. *Write a cohesive script*
   a. Introduce drum major, dancers, majorites etc.
   b. Identify band and script theme.
   c. Recognize visitors.
   d. Be certain announcer does not talk beyond 30 seconds for each section.

4. *Decide on the basic structure of the show*
   a. If show is written for *drills* recall hand flash, instrument variations, step change, fast breaks etc.
   b. Shows with a *theme* should have formations with some animation or formations with very simple lines. Keep in mind ability of group you are writing for.

    c. *Pageantry* shows use special effects such as props, balloons, fireworks, lights. Check budget and size of props to fit field. Check catalogues for costumes. Use bright colors.

    d. *Combination* show uses all available techniques to some degree. Watch length of show.

5. *Humor*
   a. Use in animated formation
   b. Audience participation
   c. A surprise climax
   d. As a major theme

6. *Element of Surprise*
   a. Check half-time supply catalogue for props
   b. Cloaked costumed figure
   c. Unusual climax
   d. Gift box unwrapped
   e. Unfurling a giant banner
   f. Bubble machine, released balloons, fireworks
   g. Flags
   h. Audience with a guest

7. *Using groups in addition to band*
   a. Pom pom girls, dancers, choir, jazz band, clowns, costumed pageantry groups, guest bands
   b. Suggest possible costuming, color staging
   c. Suggest spot for group, preferably in front of band near stands

8. *Dramatic entrance*
   a. Choose appropriate fanfare from tapes
   b. Unique entrance with at least two changes of pattern before reaching fifty yard line
   c. Keep ideas simple for *PRECISION* sake

9. *Visitor Section*
   a. Arrange to have visitor's school song played
   b. Use a school identification letter or imaginative formation
   c. Add a humorous note in script to draw the visitors into a sincere welcomed feeling
   d. Use props, twirlers, many pom pom girls, etc. for variety

10. *Change of pace*
    a. If using theme change speed with precision drill or dance routine
    b. Watch musical selections, be sure not to schedule two slow numbers or two fast selections together
    c. Change marching stride (i.e. stiff leg, knee bends, shuffle)
    d. Suggest step length, speed of step, type and height

11. *Segue*
   a. Be consistent throughout show as to style of segue
   b. Use squads, scatter, follow the leader technique
   c. Suggest drum cadence or musical selection during segue

12. *Climax*
   a. Tie in theme for announcer
   b. Use element of surprise, humor, audience participation
   c. Unveil major prop
   d. Exit fast

EVALUATION

Half-time shows which are written by gifted-creative students work well in an independent study curriculum, enrichment, and an extra-credit program. When working with a creative project of this nature it is very difficult to evaluate because of the amount of variables involved. The greatest compensation is to have a show performed. Working the shows as an extra-credit project releases the student from the strain of a grade but yet guarantees a better average when added to total musical performance evaluation at semester's end. This non-graded attitude has not deterred students from submitting shows for the project. Creating a show from paper to performance has its own unique value.

Some form of evaluation feedback still must be made by the director after reading shows. It is simple for the experienced director to pick out a winning show, but if the student has a question, suggest going back to the checklist for developing a good show. The director's form of evaluation, so that the student knows the show has been read and considered, must be in the structure of a small paragraph as:

> *Dawn J: Your show has many good ideas but the theme Indian is overworked and special effects using chemicals for fire would require a giant caldron and a great amount of chemical. More contemporary music should have been considered. We can't use the show in its present form but the entrance is excellent and shall be attached to the September half-time show with credit line to you!*

Use brief paragraphs such as this for describing and summarizing the show results and type them on a copy to be reviewed ONLY by those that did submit the shows. Some students are quite sensitive about other pupils reading comments. Always remember to say something POSITIVE along with the negative in every show submitted.

EDITING AND PRODUCTION

No show, no matter how creative can be produced without editing. The student must fully realize that writing half-time shows is a new experience and the expertise lies with the director. The usual pitfalls a director may experience is the conservativeness of the students. No matter how contemporary they appear, the ideas will often be stilted at first until they feel an openness and confidence in making suggestions to the director. They seem to want to stay away from juvenile themes as a facade to sophistication. They fear looking childish.

Positive peer feedback is very essential and negative peer criticism can be controlled by avoiding any criticism verbally until after presentation of the show. Then it should be in a controlled classroom situation. Warn students beforehand that any suggestions made for the show's improvement during rehearsal must be made directly to the music director and only positive statements will be accepted.

Technical aspects such as music tempo, instrument placement, must be arranged by the director. Be certain to have an experienced announcer rehearse with the band and drum major. Place the gifted-student in the press box with you to work out any voice inflection or desired effect. Often the view from the stands can suggest editing on the spot by the gifted-student.

The night of production, be certain that the aisles near the football field are cleared by the guards. Any negative comments made by sideline students during the band's lineup destroys concentration. The director or an audio visual person should take video tape during performance. If need be, purchase video tape for working use of this nature. Try to pick up as much music and applause as possible. Take the video-tape from the fifty yard line, outside the press box, standing on the very top bleacher.

VIDEO-TAPE ANALYSIS AND PLAYBACK

At first rehearsal after actual performance, replay video tape. Compliment the writer on a fine show and then go about analyzing for possible improvements of the band for future shows. Remind students that both positive and negative criticism is desired. The greatest feedback that has ever been experienced is when the band was so pleased with the show and performance that applause came spontaneously during playback. You know then that your teaching is coming across.

Before reviewing the tape write the following checklist on the board to promote thinking during the playback:

CHECKLIST

1. Was the entrance fairly effective? How could it have been improved?

2. Was there precision in the segues?

3. How can we improve the section recognizing our visitors? Was this segment well-received by the visitors? Look at the faces in the stands.

4. Was the music prepared enough or could another selection have been used more wisely?

5. Did we see precision in marching throughout the entire show?

6. Could formations be read easily?

7. How much applause did the show receive from the audience?

8. Did the props go off well? How could they have been improved?

9. Did the fanfare come off clearly? Were the pom pom girls, cheerleaders, twirlers coordinated with the style of the show?

10. What section in the band needs more practice?

11. Any comments that you have heard from the audience after performance?

12. Was there enough color on the field?

13. Did the show have an effective climax?

14. Would you rate the show and performance: Excellent, Fair, Poor.

After evaluation, be sure to date the show and place your rating along with the bands. Star excellent shows and repeat in a few years.

---

[14]Lee, Jack, "Modern Marching Band Techniques," Hal Leonard Music, Winona, Minn., 1955, pp. 54, 55.

CHAPTER 4

Using Gifted Students in a Multi -Media Approach to Music Appreciation Class

When the words Music Appreciation are uttered, the mind envisions yards and yards of records and tapes with students busily trying to identify musical themes, form, structure and other technical aspects. Although one cannot deny the value of such dedicated study, today's students deserve enrichment without relying on the fountainhead of knowledge, the music teacher. A very fine way to enrich Music Appreciation classes is through the use of gifted and gifted-creative students as resource people. In order to accomplish this, the student must be instructed in what shall be referred to as *"telescopic curriculum."*

This telescopic curriculum is structured into three parts. The main and largest body encompasses students in a Music Appreciation class. The instructor will use basic textbooks, records and audio-visual material that have been comfortably used in the past and will use the technique best suited to teach the major facts and objective understanding.

The second part of the curriculum concerns itself with the gifted-creative student and helps the teacher direct these students into meaningful experiences through slides, script presentation of major composers and their works.

The third and final part of the telescopic curriculum deals with the smallest number of students, those who are highly gifted and in need of developing their 'critical thinking' capabilities. Often this area is quite neglected until students reach the university. Unfortunately many of our gifted students do not extend their desire to continue study, so the need to develop this area of thought is critical.

All these parts fit naturally into the largest segment of Music Appreciation so that this curriculum is not set apart separately from the main stream of learning. These projects are very easy to direct because during the time the instructor is teaching the class, the gifted student is released from class to go to the library or A.V. room to prepare his slides, script or review books for critical analysis. During the time the gifted students are absent from class, the teacher continues as if they were present. A tape recorder is set up to play for fifty minutes so that the gifted students may catch up on class lectures anytime at home if he chooses to do so. At the conclusion of the class, the instructor merely takes the tape off the machine and dates the lecture. In this manner the absent students need not miss the sample of music analysis or pertinent information presented.

The music teacher need not set up the tape but should appoint a student in the class to do this. If a particular day arrives when six or seven gifted students would be working in the A.V. room or library, then the teacher says to a specific student at the beginning of the period, "Taping today John."

Naturally it would be inadvisable to tape for only one student, rather try to set up some type of schedule beforehand when a group may be out for that period. When the tapes are to be taken out and played back, the same student that was in charge of taping should be the librarian. Encourage listening to the tapes as a group, perhaps at someone's home.

These tapes are particularly helpful to the class as well. If students in the class have had difficulty understanding analysis of a particular work in the lecture, the tape is helpful for review.

TAPE CARREL USE

Another method which works well is to 'can' Music Appreciation programs ahead of time and place them in the library's

Figure 2

**Tape carrel for music appreciation
and comparative arts courses**

retrieval system. The system consists of twenty-four or less carrel stations which are equipped with stereo earphones with individual volume controls. Music Appreciation analysis is programmed on the system for each week. Have the week's program posted in each booth as well as in the music classroom's bulletin boards. Make certain that directions concerning the use of the system are found in each carrel.

Usually the department chairmen handles this procedure for scheduling with the librarian. The tape decks are controlled by a switch located near the carrels to allow complete playing of each cassette tape beginning each hour. The tapes automatically rewind for reuse. This listening procedure is excellent.

Recently a survey was taken in a large high school during a twenty-day period which showed one thousand thirteen earphones circulated for an average of 50.65% per day listening. Music teachers can benefit greatly from this listening trend if they use the carrels properly and avoid the pitfalls of student check-out procedures.

PROPER CHECK OUT TAPE PROCEDURE

A good policy to follow in checking out tapes is to sign for earphones by number and use the listening booth with the same number. I.D. cards given to the librarian are a guarantee that the earphones will be returned in good condition. Along with the earphones the students receive a slip to complete that will let the librarian know what program they have listened to the longest. In this manner the music teacher can determine what tapes are most popular not only with Music Appreciation students but with the student body as well and can determine future 'set-up' procedures.

HOW TO MAKE A TAPE

After the gifted student becomes familiar with library use and carrel listening, instruction should begin on making original tapes. Have your Audio-visual director tape the procedure for making a tape. Illustrate the good and bad examples of the use. These tapes should be accompanied by worksheets to be completed by students as they are listening. Gifted students are quite adept at teaching themselves how to tape.

When the mechanics are learned, the gifted student then can proceed to coordinate music tape samples of the composer's work and coordinate with the slides that are prepared.

HOW TO MAKE A TAPE WORKSHEET

1. Place recorder upon table. Avoid blocking cooling vents on bottom or sides of machine with any obstacles such as paper.

2. Plug in power cord and turn on machine.

3. Put the empty take-up reel on spindle on the left of machine thread. If using cassette, snap in tape cartridge. Dull side of tape should face the recorder front and playback heads.

4. Press button for play and turn on volume, if you hear nothing you may have a new tape. If something is on tape erase by pushing play and record button and allow to play out in a quiet room. This procedure will avoid having to record over distortion of voice or music.

5. Rewind tape and this time adjust controls properly. Do a little experimenting with volume levels. Plug in microphone.

   a. Check the lighted circle with wedge-shaped light. As you record notice how the edges of the wedge close or open as you are speaking. Adjust volume so that the wedge narrows but doesn't completely close if volume is very loud.

   b. Notice the dial with a needle which swings left to the right. This needle should move as you record but not swing completely to the right.

   c. If using earphones listen for distortion, this is an indication that volume is too loud.

6. Check again to see if microphone is securely in the jack. Tape should be taut between the reels. Don't hold microphone closer than three inches from your mouth. Speak naturally.

7. If recorder has a pause or instant-stop button take note how it works during playback.

8. Place the record player about a foot to the right of the tape recorder for easy accessibility to record change. Remember when taping music set the tape player at 7 1/2 ips.

9. Use a 5 inch 600 foot length reel which will last thirty minutes. If you use the 3 3/4 ips setting for speaking remember to switch back to the 7 1/2 ips for recording music.

10. Experiment with taping. If the acoustics of the room or outside noises mar the recording, then adjust equipment to a quieter part of the room and experiment with holding the microphone closer to the record player. Remember experiment BEFORE doing a complete tape.

11. DO NOT place bits of paper in the tape reel to denote start of tape or to indicate placement of musical samples. Mark the top of the tape, shiny side, with different color felt pens. Coordinate this marking with the number on the index dial. Note line color and number on an index card with a note of music or speaking as a directional indicator.

12. After recording is completed push stop control. Watch tape, be sure it is taut not loose before rewinding or it will snap and break when recorder is set for rewind.

13. Remove reel or cassette cartridge. Remove plugs. Put cover on machine.

14. Take reel or cartridge and label with name, subject content, date, course title.

CHARTS

After the gifted student can comfortably make a tape, charts should be set up in the music room giving a panoramic view of the music period to be studied. Not only does this reinforce the class understanding as a whole, but the charts can be used for the gifted student in determining which composer or music will hold particular concentration for independent study. Although each music teacher has his own favorite set of charts, a useful series is:

MUSICGRAPHS by Martin M. Stellhorn
P.O. Box 704
Tempe, Arizona
85281

CHART 1—1890-1970 is an integration of Post-Romanticism Individuals, Impressionism, Classicism, and an interweaving Expressionism, Primitivism and Revolution.

CHART 2—1810-1890 Romanticism

CHART 3—1740-1830 Viennese Classicism, Early Classicism

CHART 4—1600-1750 Baroque Music

CHART 5—1400-1600 Renaissance Music

CHART 6—800-1300 Medieval Music

CHART 7—600 BC-600 Ancient Music

CHART 14—600-1600 Romanesque, Gothic, Renaissance Music

CHART 15—1600-1800 Baroque, Viennese Classicism, Rococo Music

CHART 16—1800-1950 Romanticism, Classicism Music

(Cost: Charts 1-7, $4.50 per set, $1.00 per single chart, $4.00 per set in quantities of ten or more sets. Charts 14-16, $2.50 per set, $1.25 per single chart. $2.00 per set in quantities of ten or more sets.)

CHART ANALYSIS

It is easy to identify the major figures such as: Bach, Mozart, Haydn, Gluck, Handel, Beethoven and Schubert. Encouragement should be extended to take in less popular musicians such as; Spohr, Spontini, Cherbubini, Clementi, Viotti, Mehul, Monsigny, Dittersdorf, Boccherini, Paisiello, Scarlatti, Cimarosa, Piccinni, Sacchini, Sarti, Stamitz, Wagenseil and many more.

Point out that the French and American revolution occurred during this time. How did this affect the composers? What was Ben Franklin's response to Gluck's "Alceste" in Paris? These are just some lead questions a music teacher may use to stimulate thinking for developing ideas for a slide project. Any of the charts will arouse curiosity in the student.

Have the gifted student choose a subject to research. If the subject is a major figure, expect twice the amount of slides since information would be easier to procure. If a student chooses a minor figure, such as those in small print, only seven slides should be required because of the amount of searching required to uproot necessary material.

Structure the curriculum so that a gifted student can take notes and ideas from the chart itself in order to formulate an outline of ideas to direct learning about his subject as thoroughly as possible. A music teacher need not spend an entire class session explaining the chart but may refer to timely illustrations to support lecture information. It is the responsibility of the gifted student to glean knowledge on their own.

SLIDE PREPARATION

Before the student begins the technical aspects of taking colored slides from magazines, books or other resource material, the focus must be on what subjects to take. Make a checklist for slide suggestions containing the following:

SLIDES OF INTEREST FOR MUSIC APPRECIATION PROJECT

Slides of:

1. Composer
2. Family

3. Best friend
4. Birthplace
5. Overview of country where his most popular work was written.
6. Famous people composer related with; Kings, Popes, Artists, Writers, Other Composers.
7. Favorite recreation, or recreational location
8. Hobby
9. Mode of dress for time in history.
10. Children
11. Famous building where composer frequented.
12. Sample of musical score
13. Location where composer spent most of his life.
14. Place of death
15. Gravestone
16. Memorial

This list is in no way encompassing and leaves much for flexibility. No gifted student should be allowed to make less than seven slides for the project. After the student has fairly in mind what subjects he will choose, then a list of goals and objectives must be submitted so that slides become more than pictures. This is best handled in coordination with the script. However, it is wise to stress *'objectives'* when slide subjects are suggested, so that the art form of slide making isn't replacing instructional content. If a teacher feels a need to review procedures for determining educational objectives a good resource is a paperback: PREPARING INSTRUCTIONAL OBJECTIVES by Robert F. Mager, Fearon Publishers, 2165 Park Boulevard, Palo Alto, California 94306, $1.75.

SLIDE SET-UP

Almost any 35mm single-lens reflex camera can photograph colored slides from magazines or books. Avoid using supplementary lenses as they require exposure adjustments and are difficult to use. Most audio-visual departments have a close-up copying device set-up which merely mounts the camera on a post and the camera is then adjusted according to needed height on this post for taking the picture.

Those who wish to purchase a camera that can do this type of work should consider the Zeiss Ikon Contaflex Super B with the Leica close-up copying device. Most cameras work well but be certain that the film used is colored and fresh. The student should

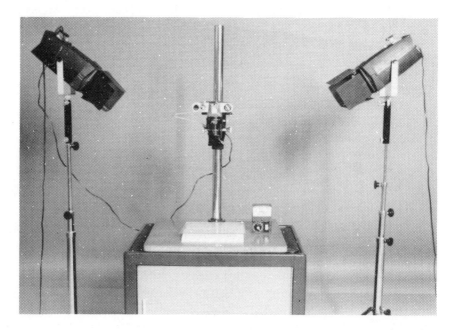

Figure 3
Making slides from book illustrations

print on white paper with one inch black India ink letters; a title card giving his name, composer, and date of the project for identification slides. Photograph this title card along with the book illustrations, the magazine, post card or any other matter that is to be used for the project. *Caution the students not to infringe on the copyright of artistic or other illustrations but to request permission for this type of project from the publishing company of the book from which the illustration is being used.* If permission becomes a hindrance an opaque projector can serve almost as well.

When the slides are developed, place on a view finder and have the student tape with yellow photograph tape on the rough side of the transparency any white borders or distracting light which detracts from the finished slide projection. If the student has been selective, the success of clear illustrations will be quite obvious. In no way should the music teacher feel that he must be the solo coordinator of this segment of the project, but should rely on his audio-visual director as a resource person. Use one or two class periods for the illustration project. During the lull between slide processing, the student should begin script concentration.

SCRIPT PRESENTATION

Before preparing a script one must become aware that behavorial objectives must be met. In this type of project, the students best understand behavioral objectives that have an attitude or factual concept. The slide together with the script should change an existing attitude. One outstanding slide project on Mozart began its behavioral objective in this manner:

When one speaks of Mozart, the vision is of a little boy in a velvet suit performing for the King of France. Although this was a fact, Mozart was much more. He wore velvet suits as a youngster, but died a pauper in an unknown grave. For his work he was given a gold watch, but had little money to live on. Let us not be deceived by that velvet suited picture frequented at the Palace of Versaille; Mozart's birthplace was indeed humble.

The student then went on to show slides of the inside of Mozart's home, a picture of him in Versaille, his works, the small cabin where he wrote *The Magic Flute* and slides which revealed the underlying theme of his objectives.

A factual behavorial objective would be a picture of a memorial, Mozart's friends, or sample of his written work. If students are having difficulty formulating objectives or the script, the music teacher will find the sample objectives and sample script helpful if duplicated and used as handouts.

SCRIPT SAMPLE

The music teacher may question the nature of the sample script since it does not depict the musical figures and slides needed in the Music Appreciation course. It was found that students copied the script style instead of developing original thoughts. By contrasting the script into a completely different area and developing sample slide sets of China, the points were perceived, and the gifted student was then forced to think of script and objectives in musical terms without copying. The sample script on China and the suggested slide titles were developed by a gifted girl for an elementary school social studies class.

Step 1. Behavioral Objective of China Slide Project

After viewing the slides and hearing the script on China, class members should be able to write a paragraph incorporating at least three basic concepts that the slides have presented. Members of the class must be able to write at least one solution or suggestion to the problems discussed in the script.

Step 2. Slide Set Introduction Written by Gifted Student

When one speaks of China, the picture that comes to mind is millions of slant-eyed, yellow-skinned, rice-eating people living in shacks. In reality China is a world power. The national language today is Mandarin which has enabled the governing people to communicate.

The Yangtze River has provided water for drinking, washing and most of all a main trade route. Because people from other countries have intermarried the characteristics we commonly attribute to the Chinese no longer exist. China has skyscrapers and many wealthy people. Presently they have had a border war with Russia. Because the communist government in China is so unlike the United States, they view us as imperalists and evil people.

Step 3. Slide Titles and Slide Script

1. TITLE SLIDE showing students name, subject and date.
2. SLIDE SHOWING PEOPLE ON STAIRS GOING TO SAMPAN.
SCRIPT: There are many stairs in Chinese cities because China is very mountainous. These people are taking vegetables from the Junks or sampans to the market square for sale. Why do you think these people are carrying the vegetables in bamboo baskets instead of paper bags? What are they eating?
3. SLIDE: MAP OF CHINA
SCRIPT: The Yangtze is the main river of China. China's closest neighbors are Mongolia and Russia to the North, Japan and Korea to the East.
4. SLIDE: SAMPAN AND JUNKS
SCRIPT: Chinese use boats called Sampans and Junks to move cargo down the river. Bamboo poles are used to move these boats because of the many levels of the Yangtze river. When the Yangtze is low, Chinese gather natural chemical called brine from it. What do they use brine for? What do American's use brine for?
5. SLIDE: MASSES OF PEOPLE WITH MODERN BUILDINGS IN BACKGROUND.
SCRIPT: There are 800 million people in China and this has caused our population experts much concern. Do you know why? Notice the many modern buildings in the background. China will soon be a major world power. How could we help feed China? Why should we?

6. SLIDE: SMALL CHILD ON SAMPAN
SCRIPT: This small boy is helping his father lay the clothing out to dry on their Sampan home. This boat is quite a nice mobile home and when the waters of the Yangtze get too high it floats to another place without too much trouble. Their home is where the boat sets.

7. SLIDE: SMALL GIRL AND MOTHER WAITING FOR A BOAT
SCRIPT: This girl is waiting for the ferry boat to take them home. We can tell that she is quite wealthy because of the rickshaw chair in the background that they have just stepped out of. Only people of wealthy means ride in this type of chair. Notice the little girl's dress and ribbons. Does she look American?

8. SLIDE: GROUP OF RUSSIAN SOLDIERS BEFORE THE EMBASSY
SCRIPT: These large group of Russian soldiers are before the Chinese embassy. Do you know why? Russia, Mongolia, and China are quarreling over border rights.

The sample script just presented is a good one because it gets the audience involved and forces the observer of the slides to think and ask direct questions. The essence of a good script is to avoid wordiness or obscure language. Make certain students avoid the trap of merely presenting descriptive slides. A good slide and script presentation must force the audience to think.

Step 4: Terminal Behavior Test

SIMULATED TEST OF CHINA SLIDE UNIT:

1. Why do the Chinese and Russians quarrel? Have the Chinese fought with other countries? Which ones? Why?
2. Why do the people in China look like us?
3. What do the Chinese eat?
4. What is the main river in China called?
5. How can the United States help China's population problem?
6. How can the United States keep China from quarreling?
7. How has language prevented China from growing technologically?
   Is there a solution to the language problem? What is it?
8. What are Chinese boats called? Why don't they have motors on them?
9. When the main river in China is low, what is the natural preservative for keeping food fresh called?
10. What countries are neighbors of China?

Step: 5 Coordination

The final step is to coordinate script, slides and a tape analysis of at least three works of the composer as to structure, form and content. How does his work distinguish itself from others? How can we tell the difference between the three works presented? Use this explanation and tape with a sample slide of the composer's manuscript or slide of composer.

To this point the teacher is quite aware that stress has not been on the Music Appreciation segment with tape analysis. Basically, this was done to eliminate repetition and infringement on the teachers expertise in conducting his own class on music analysis. After a few months in class, the gifted student should be able to pick up the basic technique of analysis and go forth to analyze the works on his own, or through the use of Music Appreciation records in the library.

Quite often the slide project will be going along smoothly when the teacher is suddenly faced with a very accelerated gifted student who has already completed the slide, script and tape project and needs more instructional direction. A temptation is to give more of the same, which can be very detrimental. It is advisable at this point to refer to the *"telescopic curriculum"* part three.

CRITICAL ANALYSIS OF BIOGRAPHICAL MATERIAL

In the third area of the telescopic curriculum, the gifted student is taught to analyze books. Often this segment of the learning process is grossly neglected until college. The gifted student's accelerated thought process need not require hours of preparation on the music teachers part. To truly challenge, these students are asked to read three different books on a particular composer's life from different points of view such as; historical, autiobiographical or biographical. A student may also choose three books from one of these categories written by three different authors in order to be exposed to three different points of view. The student is then asked to write three reports according to the worksheet suggestions.

WORKSHEET NO. 1 FOR CRITICAL ANALYSIS OF BOOK REVIEWS

READING THE BOOK

Step 1

Reading the book for review

1. Choose the book with the intent of reviewing it.
2. Pay particular attention to Introduction and Preface

3. Preface should be the clearest statement of the author's purpose in writing the book, carefully note this intent. Rewrite the intent in your own words.

4. The paragraphs should summarize the organization and add support to this purpose. Is the author getting his points across?

5. Did the author cover the scope of material he intended or did he omit something that his introduction or preface suggested.

Step 2. Taking Notes

1. As you read, take careful notes, placing the title, author, publisher, date on the top of the note paper or 4 by 5 cards. Place the page number, the quotation next to it, then your comments positive or negative regarding such statements.

2. Note particular passages which illustrate the author's purpose or those that have true significance in identifying the composer or subject. Use quotes and then make comments afterwards on whether you agree or disagree.

3. Be alert to success or failure of the author to convince you of the credibility of his knowledge. Note any controversy and add your personal comments.

4. When careful notes are taken the time will be greatly reduced in going back and finding what you remember as supportive evidence for your observation.

Step 3. Skimming and Analysis

1. After reading and taking notes on the introduction, preface and first chapter, skim the entire book to get an overview of content. You may find this book isn't worth your time reviewing.

2. After skimming the book, read with a critical eye, looking for weaknesses as well as strengths.

3. Is the author qualified to write such a book?

4. Is history accurate, descriptions clear, style cohesive? Does the author give you a feeling he KNOWS WHAT HE IS TALKING ABOUT? If so why or why not?

WORKSHEET 2. ANALYSIS AND WRITING A CRITICAL BOOK REVIEW

Step 1: Requirements of a Good Review

1. Reports what the book succeeds in doing or not doing.

2. Support with evidence how an author does or does not substantiate his views.

3. Provide enough evidence from book quotations to support or illustrate the reviewer's judgment by using direct quotations and then substantiating the judgment with critical supportive comments.

Step 2: Consider Your Reader

1. Write in the structure your reader will understand and avoid slang.

2. Avoid using slanted judgment without logical explanations of the reason for such a judgment. Try to be fair even though you may dislike the book.

3. If you are having difficulty making a judgment about the book, review the notes until such a decision can be formulated. Analyze your impressions of the book.

4. Remember the reader is an objective observer but will not tolerate judgments made without quotations to substantiate negative or positive judgment statements. Opinion is only valid when supportive evidence is given.

Step 3: Writing the Introduction

1. Leave this task until last since the opening paragraph is most difficult to write.

2. Don't begin by placing your judgment at the very beginning then try to substantiate it with paragraph upon paragraph devoted to giving reasons for your judgment.

3. Tell about the author's background, other books he has written and how he came to write this particular book.

Step 4: Writing the Body of the Review

1. Summarize the problem the author prefers to discuss and comment on its significance.

2. Use humor and anecdotes or illustrations to give the reader the mood of the author and the writer's attitude towards the author.

3. Find quotations that sum up the purpose of the book.

4. Describe the book in general to give the reader a comprehensive view of the times.

5. How does this book differ from others like it?

6. Look for author's bias and prove the point that he has a bias.

**WORKSHEET 3: MUSIC TEACHERS CHECKLIST FOR
CRITICAL BOOK REVIEW**

Basic weaknesses of a poor book review:

1. A disproportionate amount of space is taken up in an attempt to explain the action or book content so that the review is a reworded digest summation instead of a criticism.

2. Small parts are picked out of the book in quotation form to justify a particular criticism, but the criticism is too short and the evidence isn't supportive.

3. Subject digresses between illustration and tries to substantiate the reader's philosophy rather than giving his own judgment.

4. Exaggerating or presenting such a biased opinion that the style dominates the accuracy of the review.

5. Reviews so generalized that the illustrations or examples are mere statements rather than SPECIFIC evidence.

Good reviews are well thought out and reflect logical reasoning ability. The student will reflect careful structuring of the review in line with Worksheets 1 and 2.

If the statements made on the worksheets seem somewhat repetitive to you, that was the intent in order to reinforce avoidance of some of the pitfalls frequented by gifted students when writing and reading for critical review.

CHAPTER 5

Placing Gifted Students
in a Folk-Jazz Club

Black studies programs usually consist of basic literature, records, films and biographies reflecting black heritage. One cannot deny the value of such enrichment but music teachers add an advantageous twist by using these courses as a searchlight focusing on an action-oriented choir. A Folk-Jazz Choir is one way to incorporate a new course into any high school curriculum. Black students, especially, appreciate an action oriented choir and administrators enjoy the possibility of a *pilot course.*

One may wonder why just the gifted student should benefit from such an endeavor. In truth *all students* can benefit but gifted students are spotlighted in the pilot program where quality of performance is higher and the chance of getting the course approved is greater.

Beginning a *pilot course* such as a Folk-Jazz Choir exposes the need for structured curriculum for minority students. A teacher may find application for such a club so popular that limitations must be made on the number of students accommodated.

AVOIDING PITFALLS

When we speak of Folk-Jazz Music Club, we are speaking in this case of a black gospel choir. To a sophisticated audience the elimination of the word "gospel" in the title may seem superfluous. To a music teacher it has been found to be a necessity in order to avoid controversy. The curriculum should be sold as "folk."

Without an honest belief on the part of the choir director in equal curriculum opportunity for all students, this course will fail before it has a beginning. The choir director should if he is not qualified, be prepared to take a secondary role and leave the teaching to a para-professional. Responsibility for the para-professional lies with the choir director. If there is strong leadership, then the transplanting of an enriched inner-city musical form to the suburbs is an unusual and rewarding adventure.

The choir director will serve in the advisory capacity and should give flexibility of literature and teaching procedure to the para-professional. The director should also be at all large performances outside of the school such as inner-city churches or annual concerts. Lack of presence can be misunderstood as lack of interest. Public relations in such a pilot course as this is crucial.

To give the choir depth beyond performance, enrichment material in ethnomusicology should be presented to the para-professional for use. To aid in formulating such material, a list containing records, books, magazines and film are presented in the last section of this chapter.

DEFINING A FOLK-JAZZ CHOIR

Folk designates a widely different connotation in different cultures. In Europe it would mean rural music while in Southeast Asia a secular or tribal music. *Jazz* is synonomous with improvisation and creativity. Although this simple definition may suffice for students and parents; administrators, curriculum advisors, music chairman or accountability advocates require specifics.

Folk is then a stylistic form of singing using basic ballads and stories with simple guitar accompaniment. Modal harmonies would be used with melodies often singular in pitch.

Jazz is a free form of improvisation, creative in content, using swing rhythm, basic piano, bass and drums. It uses extended chords, inversions and chromatics with twelve bar blues AABA free form.

Although *Soul* or *Gospel* is not used in the curriculum title in order to avoid the possibility of controversy, it is a very integral part of the course teaching. Gospel music is derived from black churches using simple harmonies 12 measures in length and 4/4 time with free elisions referred to as blues. *Soul* is a direct derivative of gospel music with urban blues and rhythm again using a 12 bar form like jazz but occasionally with static riffs and pedal points. It uses loud basic texture with much energy and syncopation.

Add them all together and you have an in-depth definition of Folk-Jazz Choir. After defining the course the necessary forms must be filled out and presented to administration for consideration.

FORMS FOR DEVELOPING A FOLK-JAZZ CHOIR

Instructions for Filling out Club Request Form

1. Fill out club application form accurately and completely.

2. Return the completed application form to the Student Activities office.

3. When the Student/Faculty committee is ready to decide on club application, a representative or representatives will be called to sit in on the meeting to answer any questions. Please indicate the names of what representative you would like to send to the meeting by writing name on the back of the application form.

CLUB APPLICATION REQUEST FORM

(High School's Name) _____

School Year _____

Date
Submitted _____

GENERAL INFORMATION

1. Club's name:

2. Organizational date of club _____
Month   Date   Year

3. Sponsor's name _____

4. Club size _____ .

5. Club purpose:

6. What are requirements for membership:

7. How and when are members selected:

8. Meeting days: _____.
              Date   Time   Place

9. Names of club officers and official titles:

10. Do these officers meet separately?   When?

ELECTIONS

1. How are officers elected and when?

FINANCES

1. Estimate financial needs for the coming year:

2. List fund raising projects that will currently be run and approximate date of same:

3. What will be the use of these funds?

ACTIVITIES

List major activities that are being planned for the coming school year:

CLUB CONSTITUTION

If your club application is approved by the Student/Faculty Committee, a constitution will be required. Your constitution should contain:
    a. Goals
    b. Membership and participation policies
    c. Fund raising and financial policies

    d. Officers and their duties

    e. Standing committees and their duties

    f. Major activities and projects

PILOT COURSE FORM

Date:

PROPOSAL FOR A PILOT COURSE (Vocal Music)

TITLE: Folk Jazz Music Choir

MEETING TIME: Two 45-minute periods per week (out of school, Monday and Thursday.)

INSTRUCTORS NAME:

INSTRUMENTS NEEDED: Piano and organ if possible

MATERIALS NEEDED: Music to be purchased out of school budget, recordings, films, mimeographed questionnaire, part-time use of video tape, books from library on ethnomusicology.

SELECTIVITY: Voice and auditions open to anyone interested.

COURSE CONTENT: Membership is open to all students. Various ethnic styles of music will be taught. Solo and ensemble work will be emphasized. Improvisatorial techniques and creative expression will be concentrated on relinquishing traditional techniques for free flowing development.

_____

MUSIC DIRECTOR'S SIGNATURE

PARTICIPATION FORM FOR THE FOLK-JAZZ CHOIR

Date _____

Dear Parents:

_____ High School proudly announces the formation of a Folk-Jazz Choir. This is something unique and will be used as a pilot study for development of future curriculum. The choir will rehearse every Monday and Thursday from 3:20 P.M. until 5:30 P.M. in the choir room. Student transportation will be provided by an activity bus.

    We required the signature of a parent or guardian of all students participating in this new choir. The signature of the parent or guardian is

necessary as consent for the student to assure that he or she will be active in the Folk Jazz choir for the duration of the school term. The para-professional teacher who will be conducting this choir is Mr., Mrs., Ms _____.
Choir will be limited to the first fifty students.

Sincerely,

_____

-- Chairman of the Music Department --------------------

My _____ daughter, son, will be able to participate in the Folk Jazz choir. He or she will be committed for the duration of the school term.

PARENTAL OR GUARDIAN
SIGNATURE _____.

Date: _____.

ADMINISTRATIVE QUESTIONS CONCERNING
THE FOLK-JAZZ CHOIR

The following list of questions are submitted for the music administrator's careful attention. Preparation in answering these questions may sufficiently prepare the music teacher for possible administrative confrontation.

1. Will the choir represent the school in the same capacity that any other school-sponsored club would such as *Madrigals, Clefs etc.?*

2. Who will determine when the programs go before the public, the music chairman, choir director, activities chairman, principal or all?

3. Should this group be approved as a school club first, as a non-credit pilot experimental choir, or as part of the music curriculum?

4. If the choir plans to meet financial obligations through fund-raising projects, should the music chairman or choir director receive clearance from the activities director and principal as to avoid too many fund-raising drives which may conflict with other departments?

5. Would it be necessary to have a staff member of the music department present at the rehearsals of the choir? At what time must a staff member be present?

6. If a staff member is used in a capacity as choir director, will the school board pay extra compensation for such an arrangement?

7. Will the school insurance cover the para-professional instructor or must that instructor cover himself?

8. If a staff member chooses to be an instructor for the choir, could that member be released from study-hall time and rehearse the choir instead?

After the forms have been completed and submitted to administration, the next step is to wait for approval. A capsule definition will then be needed for the club in the curriculum handbook. Use the following information as reference:

FOLK-JAZZ CHOIR DESCRIPTION
FOR CURRICULUM HANDBOOK

COURSE	FOR	CREDIT	PREREQUISITES AND RECOMMENDATIONS
Folk and Jazz Music Choir	*9, 10, 11, 12*	*None*	*Audition (Open to anyone interested)*

Membership is open to all students and various ethnic styles of music will be taught. Much solo and ensemble work will be emphasized. The greatest attribute of the course is the use of improvisational techniques. While vocal experiences in our present curriculum emphasize the re-creation of music, our pilot course would encourage the student to improve on existing melodies and harmonies. In essence, we then would embark in the area of creativity. Ethnomusicology will also be stressed.

INSTRUCTOR SELECTION

The success of the pilot course is dependent on the proper selection of the music teacher for the Folk-Jazz Club. Probably few music teachers can qualify to teach the improvisation, gospel approach to a choir unless they have been schooled in the black churches. When we refer to *'soul'* we say a teacher trained in this way would help to assure the success of this pilot. The music director, therefore, would most likely look within the black community for a para-professional who would be willing to teach a group of choir students. To obtain a helpful list of names, ask black teachers, students and ministers for suggestions. The music administrator should talk to the para-professional on the phone and then send an application form to obtain qualifications for teaching. The most complete form together with a verbal survey as to popularity of such para-professional is adequate to get the job accomplished. Take a verbal survey of various black students in many classes or choirs. Ask the questions; Have you ever sung under Mr. or Mrs. _____ at your church? Would you enjoy singing under him or her in a course? Whom would you suggest as a director for the Folk-Jazz Club?

After listing various candidates, mail the application form to be completed along with a self-addressed envelope for rapid reply.

APPLICATION FORM FOR PRIVATE MUSIC INSTRUCTOR
FOR
_____ HIGH SCHOOL DISTRICT NO. _____

Mr.
Mrs.
Ms. _____
       Last name   First   Middle   Maiden

Street Address _____
              City   State   Zip

Telephone _____ Social Security Number _____

Birth Date _____ Place of Birth _____

Are you an American Citizen? _____

Are you married? _____ Have you ever been married? _____

Spouse's name _____ Occupation _____

Number of children _____ Ages _____

Are you in sound health now? _____

Have you ever been treated for mental illness? _____

When was the last date of your T.B. Xray? _____

Any physical defects:?

Do you wear glasses?   Is your hearing normal?

List the organizations or clubs to which you presently belong. (Mention any offices or positions of responsibility you have held in these organizations.)

_____

_____

Are you presently employed? _____ Where? _____

What position do you hold? _____

What is your business phone? _____

EDUCATION

Educational Institutions	Dates Attended	Diploma or Degree	Major & Minor

List the Private Instructors you have studied music with:

Private Instructor	City & State	Date	Instrument or Voice	Age/Range

CERTIFICATION

Kind of Certificate	Date	Issued By	Expires	Special Qualifications

Have you ever private taught before? _____

Where have you taught? How long? How many students?   What instrument or voice?

_____

_____

_____

_____

What dates, times and instruments or voice class would you prefer to teach?

_____

_____

What musical organization are you presently performing in? _____

_____

Whom are you presently taking lessons with? _____

_____

Were you ever in the military service? _____

Do you agree to abide by the rules and regulations of School District _____ and realize that any questionable moral behavior, drug association, profanity or abuse of school property may subject you to immediate dismissal by the Chairmen of the Music Department together with the Principals? _____

REFERENCES

Two professional, and one personal, please.

NAME	ADDRESS	PHONE	POSITION OR OCCUPATION

If you have answered the questions to the best of your ability and agree to the terms in the above statement and wish to become a private music instructor for District _____, please sign.

_____

Signature

MONETARY COMPENSATION FOR PARA-PROFESSIONAL

As long as a club or pilot course costs the school board little or nothing, the possibility for acceptance is almost assured. The plague of music personnel is just where and how to obtain necessary funds. Resource persons are music and athletic directors who normally have a file on potential fund raising projects. List of saleable items or imaginative approaches are almost endless. In fund-raising selection remember the vehicle for success is C-A-R-S: CONSUME, AMUSE, REPLACE, SECURE.

CONSUME

The favorite of most fund-raising organizations is to sell eatable or disposable items. Proper placement of personnel is most essential along with the weather or event. Check factory shift release times, athletic events, concerts, contests, parades, plays, firework displays, scout campouts, or any community event which will have large groups of people to approach. If door-to-door sales are preferred, avoid the week just after a holiday as well as income tax time or school entrance expenses. Watch temperature, the body craves more food in cold temperatures or after strenuous exercise. Sales have been notably good in football stands after the concessions ran out of food or after a large swim meet.

If the school is on split-shifts, sell to supplement cafeteria fare. Make it fresh, good and easy to handle. Avoid expense of paper plates or cups but if they are needed, use the smallest possible size.

AMUSE

People enjoy being entertained so take advantage of this by performing concerts out of the ordinary, perhaps an extravaganza combining marching, symphonic bands, some choirs and modern dancers in a field house. The more participants the greater attendance. Use a guest artist as a drawing card. Set up competitions between Jazz Bands or Combos. Don't overlook the non-musical events such as Beauty Contests, Bingo, Carnivals, Old-time Movie Night, Parties, Street Fairs and Dances.

Combining drama with music is a sure success. Invite churches, service organizations, community clubs and various P.T.A.'s to compete in a continuous performance of dramatic skits from one day to the next. Each is to have 20 minutes to perform. Winning organization gets a trophy and monetary award for their treasury. You get the profit from ticket sales. Minstrel, Variety or Children shows are also pleasing.

REPLACE

A good form of revenue is to sell new, reusable or nearly new necessary items whether it be clothing, appliances, novelties for athletic events, fad T-shirts, or child amusement items.

Think big by combining organizations for this event, using the field house or gym, then renting space to each group. Your organization gets all the admission fee. Don't overlook merchants who may rent a space for display.

If you are going to sell an item new, people appreciate buying something useful like stationery, toothbrushes, garbage bags, candles or birthday cards. When considering which item to sell, think of the longevity of the item. Christmas plastic decorations may sell well but after the first year there is little need of replacement. A wiser choice would have been fresh holly or evergreen wreaths.

SECURE

Money in the pocket with little overhead is wise. Gather patrons of the arts by selling season tickets or space in the concert program for ads. Merchants appreciate a tax deduction and so do parents. Don't overlook the possibility of legally taking necessary action to make your organization a legal non-profit organization and then sell shares to it. Parents can buy shares and deduct them for their income tax. Selling tags of your organization on the corner is also money in the bank along with good-will offerings at free concerts.

Whatever your desire in gathering funds this list of distributors will help with saleable items:

CANDY

Bowers Candies, New Albany Rd. Moorestown, New Jersey 08057
Chocolate Company of America, 910 West Van Buren St. Chicago, Ill. 60607
Gold Leaf Corp. 400 N. Portland St. Box 71, Bryan, Ohio 43506

Mason Candies, Inc. P.O. Box 549, Mineola, N.Y. 11501
Mrs. Leland's Kitchen, 1020 West Adams St., Chicago, Ill. 60607
Nestle Co. Inc. 1909 Church St. Peru, Ill. 61354
Tootsie Roll Industries, 2615 Kennedy Blvd. Jersey City, N.J.
World's Finest Chocolate, 2521 W. 48th St. Chicago, Ill. 60632

COTTON CANDY-POPCORN

Funds-A-Poppin, 5570 N. Sheridan Rd. Chicago, Ill. 60626
Gold Medal Products Co. 1825 Freeman Ave. Cincinnati, Ohio 45214

GRAPEFRUITS, ORANGES

Langdon Barber Groves, Box 1176, 2510 South Second St. McAllen, Texas 78501

ATHLETIC ITEMS
(Flags, balloons, cushions, T-shirts, novelties)

Amsterdam Company, Amsterdam, New York 12010 (catalogue)
Quality Products Inc. Box 564, Columbus, Miss. 39701
Win Craft 1124 West Fifth St. Winona, Minnesota 55987 (catalogue)

HOUSEHOLD ITEMS

Ann Elizabeth Wade, Dept. 218 M.T., Lynchburg, Virginia, 24505 (Table cloths, napkins, plates etc.)
MDS Inc., RD 2, Keystone Rd Bethlehem, Pa. 18107 (garbage bags)
Fund Raising Promotions, 145 N. Franklin Tpke, Ramsey, N.J. 07446 (Bicycle reflectors)
Fund Raising Materials, CCM Ostwald, Inc. Ostwald Plaza, Staten Island, N.Y. 10314 (Misc.)
Moffet, P.O. Box 296, Englewood, Ohio, 45322 (slippers)
Priority Mfg. Inc. P.O. Box 999, Hialeah, Florida 33011 (hostess smocks)
Revere Co. Dept. FX 92, 911 Columbia St. Scranton, Penn. 18509 (tool kits, candles)
Two Brothers Inc. Dept. TH 168, 808 Washington, St. Louis, Missouri 63101, (towels)

STATIONERY

The Giftique Co. P.O. Box 397, Buda, Illinois 61314
Jan Winters, Chestnut St. Nashua, New Hampshire 03060

Abigail Martin Products, Midwest Card Co. P.O. Box 530
1113 Washington Ave. St. Louis, Missouri 63166
Williams Stationery Co. Camden, New York 13316

CONCERTS AND FEEDBACK

A Folk-Jazz Choir will gather much attention because of the unique sound and performance. Contemporary programs daily on television use performing groups copying the soul stylist. If the choir director develops a choir as directed, very professional results will significantly add to any music program. Invitations will become numerous and the problem eventually will be how to limit the number of interested students. Concerts in churches, civic organizations or as guest artists at an instrumental music program are a sure place to check on verbal impact. Do mingle with the crowd in the stands to hear comments. Ask students their reaction. Speak to as many parents as possible about the choir. The pulse of the program lies with proper acceptance of student members and the rapport they are able to create with their audience.

Besides verbal feedback, it is helpful every four months to pass individual index cards to students and have them write their comments about the class, teacher, performances. Ask for suggestions on improvement.

USE OF VISUAL AIDES IN A FOLK-JAZZ CHOIR

VIDEO-TAPE

Video-tape is an absolute necessity when developing a teacher aid for the para-professional. Not only does the choir see how they look but can hear how they sing. Video-tape is one of the most flexible tools for pinpointing flaws in expression, appearance and over-all affect. If a video-tape machine is not available, colored movies with a coordinated tape recorder should be set up for use at least every third month.

Taping of a concert should be kept on file. Church organizations and community programs are constantly seeking something different to review in their schedule of events. Usually a short film develops interest for live performance and the Folk-Jazz choir is ready to accept invitations that normally might have been restric-

ted. If a church or organization finds the colored film entertaining,
screening of invitations is done automatically. The audience is set
for an unusual experience with little negative response.

Segregated societies often find acceptance of this type of a
singing choir very enjoyable. The breakthrough in communications
is one of the highlights of such performances.

Video-tapes and film should not be limited to taking just the
high school choir but the music director should seek out professional musical groups within the black community and inner-city.
By taping these groups with the permission of the pastor, not only
does the enrichment go beyond the classroom but public relations
are greatly enhanced.

ETHNOMUSICOLOGY ENRICHMENT

To give an indepth enrichment to the Folk-Jazz Choir, the
para-professional must be encouraged to use film, records, books
and magazines in Ethnomusicology. Concentration should be in
the area of African music specifically so that the student understands the beginnings of the Jazz-Gospel song movement. To aid
the para-professional and music director in selection of available
materials in this area, a magazine, record, film and book list are
suggested.

MAGAZINES

African Music Society, P.O. Box 138, Roodeport, Transvall, South Africa

Gospel Music Jubilee, Charlton Publication, Inc. Charlton Bldg.
Derby, Connecticut 06418

Journal of the Society for Ethnomusicology, The Society for Ethnomusicology, Room 513, 201 South Main St. Ann Arbor, Michigan 48108

RECORDS

Africa East & West IER 6751, Institute of Ethnomusicology, University of
California, Los Angeles, Calif. (African Arts Study Kit)

The African Mbira-Nonesuch 72043

Bantu Music from British East Africa Volume 10, Columbia World Library of
Folk and Primitive Music, Columic KL 213

Black Africa, Panorama of Instrumental Music, BAM LD 409A

Mbira Music of Rhodesia, University of Washington Press, Seattle, Wash.

Music of Central Africa, OCR 43

Music of the Dan Territory, Ocora, OCR 17

Nigeria-Hausa Music I-UNESCO 30L 2306

Sounds of Africa. Verve/Forecast FTS 3021

FILMS

"An African Community: The Masai" Color 16 1/4 min. *"Discovering the Music of Africa"* Color 22 min. BFA Educational Media, 2211 Michigan Avenue, Santa Monica, California 90404

"Atumpan" Color 42 min. Institute of Ethnomusicology, UCLA 405 Hilgard Ave. Los Angeles, California 90024

"Ballets of the Atlas" Black/white 10 min. Film Images, Radim Films Inc. 1034 Lake St., Oak Park, Ill. 60301

"Bali Today" Color 18 min. Hartley Productions Inc. 279 East 44th St., New York City, New York 10017

"Chopi Africa" Color 53 min. Maurice A. Machris Productions 11681 San Vicente Boulevard, Los Angeles, California, 90049

Free 16 mm. Sound Motion picture films on Folk Music and Folk Dance with rental distributions is available by writing to: Archive of Folksong, Library of Congress, Washington D.C. 20540

LIBRARY
BOOKLIST FOR FOLK-JAZZ CHOIR

Charters, Samuel B, *"Jazz: New Orleans 1885-1963,"* Oak

Cuney-Hare, Maud, *"Negro Musicians and Their Music,"* Associated Publishers

Feather, Leonard, *"The Encyclopedia of Jazz,"* New York: Bonanza Books 1960

Garland, Phyl, *"The Sound of Soul"* H. Regnery Co. 1969

Gaskin, L.S.P. editor, *"A Select Bibliography of Music in Africa,"* London: International African Institute 1965; Reprinted Boston: Crescendo Publishing Co. 1971

Geiringer, Karl, *"Musical Instruments: Their History In Western Culture from Stone Age to the Present,"* by Bernard Miall 1945 Oxford United Press

Hood, Mantle, *"The Ethnomusicologist,"* McGraw-Hill Co. 1971, New York

Jones, LeRoi, *"Black Music,"* Apollo

Jones, LeRoi, *"Blue People"* New York: William I. Morrow Co. 1963

Lang, Paul, *"One Hundred Years of Music In America,"* 1961 Schirmer

Marcus, Creil, *"Rock and Roll With Stand,"* 1969 Bacon

Shaw, Arnold, *"World of Soul,"* YA. 1969 Cowles

"Sociology and History of Popular American Music and Dance," 1920-1968, Ann Arbor Publications

"Yearbook of the International Folk Music Council" Vol. 1, 1969, Vol II 1970. Edited by Alexander L. Ringer, Urbana: University of Illinois Press

For an extensive source book of African and Afro-American materials with contributions of black musicians in concert music, theatre, gospel, blues, jazz and soul write:

Source Book, Stock No. 321-10460 $3.50 each
Music Educators National Conference
1201-16th St. N.W.
Washington, D.C. 20036

CHAPTER 6

Advancing Gifted Students
in Music Theory

The music instructor may already have determined which of his students in a Music Theory class are high convergent or high divergent thinkers. This does not, however, always determine at what level of instruction the student should be placed. If he is capable, the student will show some overt signs of creativity by directing original works within a music group, or improvising in a jazz band or choir. All these are signs but are not concrete ways of determining levels of giftedness in theory. No matter how creative a particular composition may be, there are still basic facts which a gifted student should have as tools for furthering creative ideas. Some students may have already acquired some of these facts, others may have missed the most basic and obvious music theory requirements. The instructor must not be misled by giftedness. In order to measure preparation for an accelerated Music Theory class, the music teacher must test entering behavior.

A series of entering behavior tests in Music Theory have been arranged for performing and non-performing Music Theory groups to facilitate the music teachers need for ready measurement. The performing tests have been developed for those instructors who teach Music Theory during band, orchestra or choir. The music teacher may supplement these theory tests with others that have proven valuable in determining student ability in Music Theory from previous classes.

99

One may question, *"Why bother testing entering behavior, why not just teach Music Theory?"* The answer lies in proper accelera-tion of gifted students. Tests are used as an indicator determining knowledge the student may have amassed through other classes or through self-direction. If the music teacher analyzes the deficien-cies displayed in the tests, he can carefully structure curriculum according to omissive knowledge and use lecture time more wisely. Note the frequent weaknesses displayed in the tests, headline these weaknesses such as *"Most missed melodic, rhythmic intervals,"* and then group students names within certain categories. Structure lesson plans in Music Theory according to the guidelines exposed in the tests.

TESTING ENTERING BEHAVIOR IN MUSIC THEORY

Non-Theory Class Student Tests 1,2,3

TEST 1

Use: *Master Theory Beginner's Workbook* by Charles S. Peters and Paul Yoden (Neil A. Kjos Music Co., Park Ridge, Ill.).

1. Write the beats under each note in the following.

NON-THEORY CLASS STUDENTS

Test 2 Rhythm Test

PART 1

1. $\frac{3}{4}$

6. ¢

2. $\frac{6}{8}$
Fast

7. ¢

3. $\frac{4}{4}$

8. C

4. $\frac{3}{16}$
Slow

9. $\frac{4}{4}$

5. $\frac{2}{4}$

10. $\frac{6}{8}$
Slow

PART 2 *Write Correct Notes*

11. $\frac{3}{4}$ 1 da 2 da 3 and

16. $\frac{2}{4}$ 1 and 2 and

12. $\frac{12}{8}$ 1 R 3 45 R 7 8 9 10-11-12
Slow

17. $\frac{6}{8}$ 1-2
Fast

13. $\frac{4}{4}$ 1 and-2 and -3 and-4 and

18. $\frac{4}{4}$ 1 and da 2 and

14. $\frac{3}{2}$ 1 2 3 and

19. $\frac{2}{4}$ 1-2

15. $\frac{2}{2}$ 1 e and da 2 and

20. $\frac{4}{4}$ 1-2-3-4

NON-THEORY CLASS STUDENTS

Test 3 Rhythm Test

PART 1 *Write Correct Notes*

1. $\dfrac{2}{4}$ 1 e and da 2 and and

2. $\dfrac{3}{4}$ 1-2-3

3.   1-2

4. $\dfrac{6}{8}$ slow 1 r 3 4 r 6

5. $\dfrac{12}{8}$ slow 1-2-3 4R6 7r9 10-11-12

6. $\dfrac{2}{4}$ 1 da 2 e and

7. $\dfrac{3}{4}$ 1 and-2 and-3 and

8. $\dfrac{3}{8}$ 1-2-3

9. $\dfrac{6}{8}$ 1-2-3-4-5-6

10. $\dfrac{9}{8}$ 1 r and 2 and 3

PART 2

11. $\dfrac{2}{4}$

12. $\dfrac{4}{4}$

13. $\dfrac{3}{2}$

14. $\dfrac{6}{8}$ slow

15. ¢

16. $\dfrac{2}{4}$

17. $\dfrac{3}{4}$

18. $\dfrac{2}{4}$

19. $\dfrac{4}{4}$

20. $\dfrac{3}{8}$ slow

THEORY TESTS 4,5,6 FOR MUSIC THEORY STUDENTS

Test 4 Theory Test

1. Name the flats in proper order up to six flats _____ .

2. Name the sharps in proper order up to six sharps. _____ .

3. Match the following:

C _____ 1. five sharps

G _____ 2. three flats

D _____ 3. five flats

A _____ 4. one flat

E _____ 5. two sharps

B _____ 6. three sharps

G♭_____ 7. no sharps or flats

D♭_____ 8. four sharps

A♭_____ 9. two flats

E♭_____10. six flats

B♭_____11. one sharp

F _____12. four flats

For further detailed testing use: *Master Theory Book II*, by Charles S. Peters and Paul Yoder (Neil A. Kjos Music Co., Park Ridge, Ill.).

4. Write the beats under the following *one count* rhythms,

A. _____ ♩ B. _____ ♫ C. _____ ♪♩ D. _____ ♫. E. _____ ♬♬

F. _____ ♬♩ G. _____ ♫♪♩ H. _____ ♬(3) I. _____ ♫♩

5. Write the notes and rests represented by the beats below:

$\frac{4}{4}$ _____

4   1-2 R 4   1 an 2 3an 4   1 R R 4   1 2an 3 R

$\frac{4}{4}$ _____

4   R 2an 3 R   1 e an da 2 R R   1 R 2 R 3-4   1 2 e an da 3 4

$\frac{2}{4}$ _____

4   1 R R an   R an da R an da   1 e R da 2 an   le R da 2

$\frac{3}{4}$ _____

4   R e an da 2 3   1 an 2 R an da 3 R   1 e R da 2 an 3   R anda2anda3

6. Write the beats under each note and rest:

MUSIC THEORY

Test 5

1. Name the following intervals:

   A. _____ B. _____

   C. _____ D. _____

2. For each of the following intervals, determine the scale which contains both tones. More than one scale is to be found for each interval.

   A. 1. _____ 2. _____

   B. 1. _____ 2. _____

   C. 1. _____ 2. _____

   D. 1. _____ 2. _____

3. With the note 6# as the top note of the triad, write in four parts the following chord forms:

   A. A major triad in first inversion with 5th in soprano.
   B. A dissonant triad with its third in soprano.
   C. A triad in second inversion in the key of E.
   D. A triad whose root is the mediant of a minor scale.

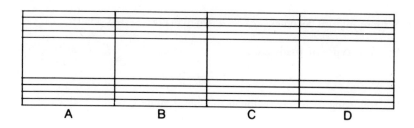

4. In which tonalities is B-flat a modal degree? A tonal degree?

_____

5. Write out the four part harmony indicated by the following figured bass.

6. Harmonize the following bass in four parts using triads in root position.

7. A major interval becomes _____ when made a $\frac{1}{2}$ step smaller.

8. A perfect interval becomes _____ when made $\frac{1}{2}$ step larger.

9. A major interval becomes _____ when made $\frac{1}{2}$ step larger.

10. A minor interval becomes _____ when made $\frac{1}{2}$ step smaller.

11. The four types of triads are _____ , _____ ,

    _____ and _____ .

12. The following triads are major in the major mode: _____ ,

    _____ , and _____ .

13. The following triads are major in the minor mode: _____ ,

    _____ , and _____ .

14. The following triads are minor in the major mode: _____ ,

    _____ , and _____ .

15. The following triads are minor in the minor mode: _____ ,

    and _____ .

16. Write the relative minor to the major keys:

    C _____ , G _____ , D _____ ,

    A _____ , E _____ , B _____ ,

    G^b _____ , D^b _____ , B^b _____ ,

    A^b _____ , E^b _____ , F _____ .

17. The three types of motion are _____ , _____ ,

    _____ .

18. The proper way to handle a tritone would be _____

    _____ .

19. Describe overlapping voices _____

    _____

    _____ .

20. Tonality is _____ .

21. Modality is _____ .

22. _____ and _____ are modal degrees.

23. The following are the names of the scale degrees:

I _____ , II _____ , III _____ ,

IV _____ , V _____ , VI _____ ,

VII _____ .

24. Interpret the F major triad in at least four tonalities:

1. _____ 2. _____ 3. _____ 4. _____

25. A $\frac{6}{5}$ inversion places the _____ of the chord in the bass.

26. A 2 inversion places the _____ of the chord in the bass.

27. A $\frac{4}{3}$ inversion places the _____ of the chord in the bass.

28. A masculine ending is _____

_____ .

29. A feminine ending is _____

_____ .

30. Write examples of the following on the back of this page.
    A. Passing Tone
    B. Auxiliary Tone
    C. Appoggiatura
    D. Suspension

31. The echappee and cambiata are used as ornamental resolutions of a suspension. Describe them:

Echappee _____ .

Cambiata _____ .

32. A $\frac{6}{4}$ chord has the _____ of the chord in the bass.

33. A 6 chord has the _____ of the chord in the bass.

34. An authentic cadence is _____ .

35. A plagal cadence is _____.

36. A half cadence is _____.

37. A deceptive cadence is _____

_____.

38. The difference between melodic and harmonic rhythm is _____

_____

_____.

39. Static harmony is _____

_____.

40. A pedal tone is _____

_____.

41. Harmonize the following soprano melody.

42. Write the voice leading rules for the following:

II-V. _____

_____.

IV-V. _____

_____.

V-VI. _____

_____.

MUSIC THEORY AND HARMONY

Test 6

1. Write the phrase below in four parts having the following pattern of harmonic rhythm and employing the harmonies suggested by the given numerals:

C Minor I V VI IV II   I V I   V

2. List eleven key interpretations of a C major triad.

A _____   G _____

B _____   H _____

C _____   I _____

D _____   J _____

E _____   K _____

F _____   L _____

3. Write out in Roman numerals the scheme of a phrase modulating in each of the following ways (four separate phrases in all), using only triads.

A. The pivot chord is II of the second key.

_____

B. The pivot chord is V of the first key.

_____

C. The modulation is to a key perfect fourth above the original key.

_____

D. The modulation is to a key a minor third above the original key.

_____

4. The inversion numbers of a dominant seventh chord are:

5. Work out the following figured bass:

6. The following is a list of dominant harmony chords. Write the correct chord tones in the key of C.

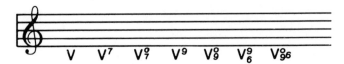

7. By changing chord tones enharmonically, find 12 key relationships to the chord B, D, F, A^b.

A _____   G _____

B _____   H _____

C _____   I _____

D _____   J _____

E _____   K _____

F _____   L _____

8. _____ is the chord tone usually omitted from the complete dominant ninth.

DIRECTIONAL TEACHING WITHIN THE CLASSROOM

A misconception among educators is that separate classes must be available to gifted students. This is not the case in Music Theory since basics are needed by all students and supplement teaching can be directed within the framework of an ordinary class. The practical goal is to establish proper levels of acceleration for gifted students from the grouping of deficiencies displayed in the tests. This is not as complicated as it may appear since gifted students need a great deal of review in basic theory. Directional teaching comes about when the teacher knows which students in the group have gifted ability and what deficiency these students may have. Rarely is there a student who has evolving proficiencies in all areas of Music Theory. If this should be the case, more composition is encouraged.

Directional teaching is very difficult to explain since it is more an atmosphere than a method. The students direct the class with the teacher as a guide. The easiest way to expose the method is to follow the steps in teaching a Gifted Music Theory Class. The emphasis is on ear-training which has proven proficient enough to prepare gifted students for college Theory classes. Through the step by step preparation, students have met with continued success.

STEP BY STEP TECHNIQUE
FOR IN-CLASS EAR TRAINING

MATERIALS NEEDED:

Piano, record player, blackboard.
Rutgers University Music Dictation Series
Music Minus One
42 West 61st. St.
New York, N.Y. 10023

BOOKS:

"Adventures in Listening" by Joseph Mechlis, Norton Press
"Harmony," Walter Piston, Norton Press
Theory Workbooks of Teachers Choice
"The Encyclopedia of Basic Harmony & Theory Applied To Improvisation On All Instruments." Vol. I, II, III by Dick Grove

Step 1.

Use Rutgers answer sheets and play them repeatedly on the piano. Play sample over more than once. Students prefer this because of the presence of sound. Continue this method until they can identify generally and specifically the intervals; major, minor, diminished and augmented.

Step 2.

Use rhythmic dictation from simple to complex again relying on Rutgers as a framework using Volume 1 on the record for review.

Step 3.

Give a simple assignment like *"Star-Spangled Banner"* or *"Happy Birthday,"* song and have students write out rhythmic patterns. Write them in concert key of Bb.

Step 4.

Give starting note and meter and have students complete melodic intervals of *"Happy Birthday,"* or *"Star-Spangled Banner."*

Step 5.

Encourage students to perform on an instrument or sing improvisationally. Jazz band, Gospel choirs or any combo that allows musicians to improvise on a theme improves ear-training dramatically. Students depend on their ear and are forced to improve in a split second time while performing.

Step 6.

Ask students to bring in a favorite record. Play the record for the class. Pick out two phrases at a time and have the students write these phrases. While the average student writes the phrases have your gifted Music Theory students accelerate by writing in harmonies and chords along with the phrases. This keeps the gifted so busy they don't have time to become bored with the class.

Step 7.

Students are to write an original melody for the class. Gifted again are not only required to write the melody but chords and harmonies. Now write some of these original melodies on the blackboard and ask different members of the class to harmonize this melody. Students are always fascinated with the great differences in harmonization possibilities.

Step 8.

For the less gifted, ask them to write only the melody line. The more gifted should write melodies, lyrics, harmonies and be able to perform them in class either singing or on an instrument.

Step 9.

Always use two textbooks for an accelerated Music Theory class one advanced and one less challenging so that students can refer to the easier one if confusion results.

Step 10.

Encourage creativity, praise liberally, correct gently and demand thoroughness of basic learning.

STUDENT SUPPLEMENTAL STUDY

If a student has performed in a jazz band, combo or choir, the ear is pronouncedly superior to a gifted student who has not been forced to improve or play by ear. Class time does not permit the individual improvement needed by the gifted student in the area of ear-training. Some may wish to go on to college realizing that their "ear" is not what it should be. These students however choose not to become part of the *'jobbing musician.'* A music teacher is often placed in a dilemma of wanting to improve the ear-training within a class but recognizes that this is an impossibility due to split sessions or overcrowded conditions. A very successful method again is to extend the classroom to the home by using Rutgers University Music Dictation Series.

Melodic dictation in the series is divided into ten sections. Each section of the Rutgers is to be studied separately. The record set for home use should be labeled and the student allowed to check it out in Music Theory class. The record is then played on a record player at home. If the student does not own a record player then the Music Department should loan a very inexpensive one for that week. After the student feels secure in his ear improvement on a particular musical section, the Rutgers test is given and graded by the music teacher at a convenient time. The student is made aware that the Rutgers' tests have been graded strictly for self-improvement and not as a grade in the class for ear-training.

RAP SESSIONS AS ENRICHMENT

Music Theory requires covering a large area of musical ground in a short period. Often the goal of obtaining knowledge somewhat loses the student in the process. A gifted student who is in a class without necessary acceleration may begin to develop into a disciplinary problem. To avoid this possibility, it is wise if one session a month is turned over to rap sessions. Set the class within a circle of chairs and begin asking questions on course content, how to improve the teaching method, what the student wishes to get out of the course and questions of this nature. The students can be very candid and the teacher may obtain invaluable insights. *It is not without warning that this procedure is suggested.*

A sensitive or fairly new music teacher may find this method an ego-devaluating procedure. When one asks for critical comments, he must be prepared for disappointment. However, in no way should the teacher allow the student to structure the course content. The basic interest is in communication, not in what is to be taught but how can a specific idea come across more clearly. Gifted students can offer excellent suggestions to less gifted students. Each student no matter how accelerated has a unique contribution to make to the class and must be discouraged from becoming too self-centered.

WRITTEN CRITIQUES

One of the favorite aids to proper student feedback is the 4 by 6 blank card. This method has proven consistently good over the years because it allows self-expression for very shy individuals or students who may have difficulty expressing thoughts verbally. If the "rap" sessions prove unproductive, use this method instead: Pass out cards and ask students to write their comments. It is interesting to see the reactions. To guide the music instructor in searching for insight into proper atmosphere for a Music Theory class, use the following examples from written critiques submitted from an accelerated group of gifted students. Instruct a class to omit signatures on the card for more honest evaluation.

STUDENT CRITICAL CRITIQUES

Student A:

The text is very good, but I think we should follow one text page-by-page mentioning the important facts only. The ear-training is great. I understand it pretty well, but I do enjoy using the time for practice, and if it helps other students more than it does me, I am willing to spend more time on this aspect. I think time should be put aside to work on individual compositions. Later let students perform their pieces, either vocal or instrumental. Also, maybe the class could do some project such as you giving us a specific song or melody and let the class work individually on arranging the piece for voice or band or small ensembles.

Student B:

We should spend more time writing music and using the book than we do the ear-training course. One of the reasons I feel a lot of us aren't doing so well is that Theory is a course that takes a lot of work and effort and if you have other interests it's very hard to understand. If I spent more time on my homework, I feel I would pass this course. I do think you are very fair as to letting us turn in homework late but we do have one grade lowered. One thing that really bothers me about the course is that I am really more worried about the grade. I wish I could think of music first and then the grade. At least you're not out to shove this course down our throats and forget about us whether we fail or not. You really want us to learn and then pass.

Student C:

I think we should spend more time on four-part harmony. It's hard to catch on fast though it's easier for some to catch on quicker. I don't think everyone understands rhythm. I like knowing what is on the test before we have it. I think once in a while we should have a whole period where we could be helped individually on a certain problem or using the period to have students help each other. I think sometimes students can get it across to each other better than a teacher or the book. I really wish we would have spent more time on four part harmony. I don't think you should lower our grade if we can't get our homework in. I think it takes longer for some people to do an assignment. I think if it happens all the time then take a few points off.

Student D:

I believe that the balance between Theory and Ear-training is very good, except that rhythms and inversions need special attention. Reading the book aloud in class is helpful because you can add to it or explain it. The ear-training records are helpful to me. I can tell that my ear is getting much better.

These are just a random sampling of comments made by gifted students about their Music Theory class. The comments speak for themselves. It is directional curriculum from the *'eye'* of the student.

The positive criticism of the class has been exposed due to the carefully created atmosphere of the teacher to allow this type of critical thinking. It is also interesting to note the underlying theme of the desire for an individualized curriculum for gifted students. Each student is accelerated at a different level and through the use of this type of written critique the teacher can structure Music Theory for the expected need rather than relying on test scores alone.

CHAPTER 7

Comparative Arts Course
for Gifted Music Students

When curriculum for a Comparative Arts course is formulated, one may be tempted to look at the list of artists, painters, musicians and interpret these as filler pages in a book. Essentially these are the very tools which support the teacher in the classroom and the use is dependent on skillful adaptation for each individual need.

In the formulation of such curriculum the mind is drawn back in time to Leonardo Da Vinci and his painting of the young St. John the Baptist. Leonardo was sixty years at the time and in his philosophical period. Essential mystical beauty seemed to be in the hand of St. John as his finger pointed heavenward. Leonardo's companions kept asking him what the finger was pointing to. To satisfy them, he finally painted a cross in the hand, transporting the nebulous art into direct communication.

So too, when Comparative Arts is taught by music people the nebulous quality becomes art in audio form. The exciting venture in teaching such a course is the amount of power the music teacher has in directing thinking to a positive plan. The student can be transported from a Social Studies class with its negative connotation of wars to positive creative element in overviewing world events, inventions and their effects on the artist, composer and writer.

The communication and cognitive cohesiveness of the curriculum lie with the instructor but the teaching and discovering of ideas remain the responsibility of the student. We use the telescopic curriculum in three parts: first the general choosing of specific comparative arts figures. Secondly we have the student outline this period in history and suggest thumbnail sketches and brief outlines as guidelines into preparing a notebook.

Third, the student passes out ditto sheets of an outline from his research to the classmates and prepares a fifteen minute speech complete with samples of the art, music, slides from the period, explaining the effect other elements such as politics, religion, war or poverty had upon the times and the artists' work. From this outline the music instructor prepares his class test.

PART I
SELECTING COMPARATIVE ARTS FIGURES, EVENTS AND INVENTIONS

One of the most frustrating problems confronting a music teacher is exactly which event or figure shall be listed to study in a Comparative Arts course. To state that this selection can require an unbelievable amount of time is an understatement. Naturally in one chapter it is almost impossible to list in all-inclusive chronology. Rather a practical selection of famous architects, composers, painters, sculptures, novelists, dramatists, poets, world events and inventions are listed.

For best results the music teacher should have these lists printed on large poster board by the print shop or done in India ink by gifted art students. To obtain a parallel concept, enter the listing and place charts side by side according to year and title. By reading horizontally the student should conceive of the world in which the artist lived. By artist we mean a general description of all famous figures in the comparative arts list.

These lists should save many hours of library research and assist the student in determining which important figures will be his selection. A figure, invention and event are to be gleaned from each list by one student and researched. To avoid change of mind, the student's name should be written beside the comparative arts figure for future reference in a teacher's notebook containing a duplicate listing.

LISTS

ARCHITECTS

Giotto 1266-1337 Italian
Brunelleschi 1377-1446 Italian
Alberti 1404-1472 Italian
Bramante 1444-1514 Italian
Michelangelo 1475-1546 Italian
Palladio 1518-1580 Italian
Bernini 1598-1680 Italian
Wren 1632-1723 British
Adam 1728-1792 Scottish

Bulfinch 1763-1844 American
Latrobe 1764-1820 American
Walter 1804-1887 American
Hunt 1827-1895 American
Jenney 1832-1907 American
Adler 1844-1900 American
Burnham 1846-1912 American

White 1853-1906 American
Sullivan 1856-1924 American
Wright 1869-1959 American
Behrens 1868-1940 German
Lutyens 1869-1944 British
Richardson 1870-1946 American
Saarinen 1873-1950 Finnish
Gropius 1883-1969 German
Mies van der Rohe 1886-1969
    German
Mendelsohn 1887-1953 German
Le Corbusier 1887-1965 Swiss
Neutra 1892-1970 Austrian
Aalto 1898-   Finnish
Stone 1902-   American
Niemeyer 1907-   Brazil
Saarinen, Eero 1910-1961 American

COMPOSERS

Dufay 1400-1474 Flemish
Obrecht 1430-1505 Flemish
Isaac 1450-1517 Flemish
Josquin Des Pres 1450-1521 French
Cabezon 1510-1566 Spanish
Morales 1512-1553 Spanish
Zarlino 1517-1590 Italian
Jannequin 1525-1560 French
Palestrina 1525-1594 Italian
di' Lasso 1532-1594 Flemish
Victoria 1540-1611 Spanish
Byrd 1542-1623 English
Gabrieli 1557-1612 Italian
Sweelinck 1562-1621 Dutch
Hassler 1564-1612 German
Gibbons 1583-1625 British
Purcell 1659-1695 British

Vivaldi 1677-1741 Italian

J.S. Bach 1685-1750 German
Handel 1685-1759 German
Haydn 1732-1809 Austrian
Mozart 1756-1791
Beethoven 1770-1827 German
Rossini 1792-1868 Italian
Schubert 1797-1828 Austrian
Berlioz 1803-1869 French
Mendelssohn 1809-1847 German
Chopin 1810-1849 Polish
R. Schumann 1810-1856 German
Liszt 1811-1886 Hungarian
Wagner 1813-1883 German
Verdi 1813-1901 Italian
Franck 1822-1890 Belgian
Bruckner 1824-1896 Austrian
Brahms 1833-1897 German
Bizet 1838-1875 French
Mussorgsky 1839-1881 Russian

COMPOSERS (Continued)

Tchaikovsky 1840-1893 Russian
Dvorak 1841-1904 Czech
Rimsky-Korsakov 1844-1908
  Russian
G. Puccini 1859-1924 Italian
Mahler 1860-1911 Austrian
Debussy 1862-1918 French
R. Strauss 1864-1949 German
Sibelius 1865-1957 Finnish
Vaughn Williams 1872-1958 British
Schoenberg 1874-1951 Austrian
C. Ives 1874-1954 American

Ravel 1875-1937 French
Bartok 1881-1945 Hungarian
Stravinsky 1882-1972 Russian
Prokofiev 1891-1953 Russian
Honegger 1892-1955 French
Milhaud 1892-   French
Hindemith 1895-1963 German
Sessions 1896-   American
Copland 1900-   American
Shostakovich 1906-1975 Russian
Britten 1913-   British
Bernstein 1918-   American

DRAMATISTS, NOVELISTS, POETS

Petrarch 1304-1374 French
Boccaccio 1313-1375 Italian
Ariosto 1474-1533 Italian
Pulci 1432-1484 Italian
Boiardo 1434-1494 Italian
Sannazaro 1458-1530 Italian
Machiavelli 1469-1527 Italian
Rabelais 1494-1553 French
Calvin 1509-1564 French
De Ronsard, 1524-1585 French
Montaigne 1533-1592 French
Cervantes 1547-1616 Spanish
Spenser 1552-1599 British
De Vega 1562-1635 Spanish
Marlowe 1564-1593 British
Shakespeare 1564-1616 British
Corneille 1606-1684 French
Milton 1608-1674 British
Moliere 1622-1673 French
Racine 1639-1699 French
Fielding 1707-1754 British
Rousseau 1712- 1778 French
Goethe 1749-1832 German
Schiller 1759-1805 German
Wordsworth 1770-1850 British
Irving 1783-1859 American
Shelley 1792-1822 British

Stendhal 1793-1842 French
Keats 1795-1821 British
Heine 1797-1856 German
Pushkin 1799-1837 Russian
Balzac 1799-1850 French
Hugo 1802-1885 French
Hawthorne 1804-1864 American
Anderson 1805-1875 Danish
Longfellow 1807-1882 American
Poe 1809-1849 American
Thackeray 1811-1863 British
Dickens 1812-1870 British
Bronte 1816-1855 British
Melville 1819-1891 American
Whitman 1819-1892 American
Baudelaire 1821-1867 French
Flaubert 1821-1880 French
Dostoevsky 1821-1881 Russian
Verne 1828-1905 American
Tolstoy 1828-1910 Russian
Ibsen 1828-1906 Norwegian
Bjornson, 1832-1910 Norwegian
Twain 1835-1910 American
Shaw 1856-1950 British
Conrad 1857-1724 Polish
Lagerlof 1858-1940 Swedish
Chekhov 1860-1904 Russian

O. Henry 1862-1910 American
Yeats 1865-1939 Irish
Galsworthy 1867-1933 British
Pirandello 1867-1936 Italian
Gorky 1868-1936 Russian
Proust 1871-1922 French
Stein 1874-1946 American
Frost 1874-1963 American
Fitzgerald 1876-1940 American

Mann 1875-1955 German
Joyce 1882-1941 Irish
Millay 1882-1950 American
Gibran 1883-1931 Lebanon
O'Neill 1888-1953 American
Eliot 1888-1965 British
Pasternak 1890-1960 Russian
Faulkner 1897-1962 American
Hemingway 1899-1961 American

PAINTERS

Limbourg 13—-1416 French
Van Eyck 1380-1440 Flemish
Fra Angelico 1387-1455 Italian
Uccello 1396-1479 Italian
Masaccio 1401-1428 Italian
Piero della Francesca 1410-1492 Italian
Belinni 1430-1516 Italian
Botticelli 1444-1510 Italian
Bosch 1450-1516 Flemish
DaVinci 1452-1519 Italian
Durer 1471-1528 German
Giorgione 1477-1510 Italian
Grunewald 1475-1528 German
Michelangelo 1475-1564 Italian
Titian 1477-1576 Italian
Raphael 1483-1520 Italian
Holbein 1497-1543 German
Tintoretto 1518-1594 Italian
Brueghel 1525-1569 Flemish
Greco, El 1541-1614 Spanish
Rubens 1577-1640 Flemish
Hals 1580-1666 Dutch
Le Nain 1593-1648 French
Poussin 1594-1665 French
Van Dyck 1599-1641 Flemish
Velazquez 1599-1660 Spanish
Claude 1600-1682 French
Rembrandt 1606-1669 Dutch
Ruisdael 1628-1682 Dutch
Vermeer 1632-1675 Dutch

DeHooch 1659-1660 Flemish
Watteau 1684-1721 French
Tiepolo 1692-1770 Italian
Hogarth 1697-1764 British
Chardin 1699-1779 French
Fragonard 1732-1806 French
West 1738-1820 American
Goya 1746-1828 Spanish
Blake 1757-1827 British
Hokusai 1760-1849 Japanese
Turner 1775-1851 British
Constable 1776-1837 British
Hicks 1780-1849 American
Audubon 1785-1851 American
Corot 1796-1875 French
Daumier 1808-1879 French
Manet 1832-1883 French
Whistler 1834-1903 American
Degas 1834-1917 French
Homer 1836-1910 American
Cezanne 1839-1906 French
Monet 1840-1926 French
Renoir 1841-1919 French
Rousseau 1844-1910 French
Eakins 1844-1916 American
Cassatt 1845-1926 American
Ryder 1847-1917 American
Harnett 1848-1892 American
Gauguin 1848-1903 French
Van Gogh 1853-1890 Dutch
Sargent 1856-1952 American

PAINTERS (Continued)

Seurat 1859-1891 French
Toulouse-Lautrec 1864-1901 French
Kandinsky 1866-1944 Russian
Matisse 1869-1954 French
Marin 1870-1953 American
Rouault 1871-1958 French
Mondrian 1872-1944 Dutch
Dufy 1877-1953 French
Klee 1879-1940 Swiss
Hofmann 1880-1966 German
Leger 1881-1955 French
Picasso 1881-1973 Spanish
Braque 1882-1963 French
Bellows 1882-1925 American
Orozco 1883-1949 Mexican
Modigliani 1884-1920 Italian
Kokoschka 1886-   Austrian

Chirico 1888-   Italian
Chagall 1889-   Russian
Ernst 1891-   German
Wood 1892-1942 American
Miro 1893-   Spanish
Nicholson 1894-   British
Curry 1897-1946 American
Shahn 1898-   American
Tamayo 1899-   Mexican
Tanguy 1900-1955 French
DeKooning 1904-   Dutch
Bacon 1910-   British
Park 1911-1960 American
Pollock 1912-1956 American
Levine 1915-   American
Wyeth 1917-   American
Rauschenberg 1925-   American

SCULPTORS

Ghiberti 1378-1455 Italian
Donatello 1386-1466 Italian
Della Robia Luca 1400-1482 Italian
Della   Robia,   Andrea   1435-1525
   Italian
Pollaiuolo 1432-1498 Italian
Verrocchio 1435-1488 Italian
Stoss 1440-1533 German
Da Vinci 1452-1519 Italian
Riemenschneider 1460-1531
   German
Michelangelo 1475-1564 Italian
Cellini 1500-1571 Italian
Goujon 1540-1562 French
Bernini 1598-1680 Italian
Coysevox 1640-1720 French
Houdon 1741-1828 French
Canova 1757-1822 Italian
Thorwaldsen 1770-1844 Danish
Barye 1795-1875 French
Greenough 1805-1852 American
Powers 1805-1873 American
Crawford 1813-1857 American

Bartholdi 1834-1904 French
Rodin 1840-1917 French
Saint-Guadens 1848-1907 American
French 1850-1931 American
Taft 1860-1936 American
Remington 1861-1909
Dallin 1861-1944 American
Maillol 1861-1944 French
Russell 1864-1926 American
Barlach 1870-1938 German
Borglum 1871-1941 American
Milles 1875-1955 American
Fraser 1876-1953 American
Brancusi 1876-1957 French
Epstein 1880-1959 American
Lehmbruck 1881-1919 German
Picasso 1881-1973 Spanish
Boccioni 1882-1916 Italian
Davidson 1883-1952 American
Mestrovic 1883-1961 Yugoslav
Hoffman 1885-1966 American
Manship 1885-1966 American
Pevsner 1886-1962 French

Archipenko 1887-1964 Russian
Arp 1887-1966 French
Zorach 1887-1966 Hungarian
Gabo 1890-   American
Lipchitz 1891-   American
Calder 1898-   American
Moore 1898-   British
Nevelson 1900-   American

Giacometti 1901-1966 Swiss
Noguchi 1904-   American
Smith 1906-1965 American
Roszak 1907-   American
Lippold, Richard 1915-
     American
Segal 1924-   American

WORLD EVENTS AND INVENTIONS

1100-1300	Crusades
1273-1806	Hapsburg rule
1300-1500	Decline of Church
1300-1650	Religious Revolt
1300-1600	Renaissance
1337-1453	Hundred Years War
1378-1417	Great Schism church lost prestige with two popes controlling
1410	Teutonic Knights of Tannenberg defeated
1414	Council of Constance voted to solve Great Schism problem
1426	Pachacutic Inca formed Peruvian Empire
1430	Mexican Empire consolidated under Aztecs
1440	Gutenberg—printing
1450	Renaissance spreads to northern Europe; Erasmus leading scholar
1452-1498	Sagonarola averts French invasion of Florence Italy
1452-1806	Holy Roman Empire ruled by Hapsburg
1453	Ottoman Turks capture Constantinople. Europe looks for overseas route to spice islands.
1454	Gutenberg uses movable type
1469	Isabella and Ferdinand marry uniting Iberia
1466-1536	Erasmus the rationalist
1469-1492	Lorenzo de Medici becomes patron of Michelangelo
1483-1546	Martin Luther
1484-1531	Zwingli gives importance to Protestantism
1485	War of Roses ended
1485-1643	Tudor Rule
1486	Cape of Good Hope discovered by Diaz
1490	Spain began Golden Age of Art and Learning beginning with Cervantes
1492-1549	Margaret of Navarre as the French patroness

WORLD EVENTS AND INVENTIONS (Continued)

1492	Columbus discovered America landing on Watling Island in the Bahamas
1493	Columbus discovers West Indian islands
1494	Italy invaded; humanistic ideas spread northward
1494-1559	Italian wars
1497	Cabot discovered Labrador
1498	Vasco da Gama sailed around Africa to India
1498	Columbus discovers South America
1500's	Spaniards—Musket
1500-1530	High Renaissance: Classical influence with importance of the individual most significant.
1501	Amerigo Vespucci explored Brazil
1502	Columbus to Central America
1508	Spaniards conquered Puerto Rico and Cuba
1509-1564	Calvin established a new branch of Protestantism with emphasis on predestination
1513	Balboa discovered Pacific Ocean, Ponce de Leon landed in Florida
1515	Francis I became King of France
1517	Luther posts 95 propositions and instigates the Protestant Revolt
1519-1521	Cortez conquered Mexico
1519-1522	Ferdinand Magellan dies during Spanish ships first voyage
1524-1525	Peasant War
1526	Huayna Capac Great Peruvian Inca dies
1529	Henry VIII's Act of Supremacy
1531-1535	Pizarro conquers Peru
1532	Machiavelli's THE PRINCE is published five years after his death
1533-1592	Montaigne sees the importance of human problems
1540	Camillo Vitelli—pistol, Italy
1543	Copernicus demonstrates earth and planets revolve around sun
1545-1563	Council of Trent
1546-1555	Schmalkaldic Wars with Lutheran princes revolting
1553-1558	Unsuccessful return of Catholicism in England under Queen Mary
1558-1603	Protestantism reestablished under Queen Elizabeth
1588	Defeat of Spanish Armada
1590	Zacharias Janssen—Compound microscope, Netherlands

1593	Galileo—Thermometer, Italy
1600-1914	Russo-Turkish War
1622-1900	Indian Wars
1607	Virginia settled Jamestown by London Co. under Capt. John Smith
1608	Samuel de Champlain founds Quebec
1618-1648	30 Years War
1619	House of Burgess founded. Wives and Negro slaves arrive in Virginia
1630	Puritans settled Massachusetts Bay
1634	Lord Baltimore settled Maryland for Catholics
1636	Roger Williams settled Rhode Island
1638	New Haven settled by Puritans
1640	First book published in America, *"Bay Psalm Book"*
1642	Blaise Pascal—Adding Machine, France
1656	Ann Hibbins hanged as a witch in Salem
1682	William Penn settles Pennsylvania
1689-1763	French and Indian Wars
1691	First post-office organized in U.S.
1692	Persecution in Salem of 16 women, 5 men hung for witchcraft
1698	Thomas Savery—Steam Pump, England
1701-1714	Succession Wars
1712	Thomas Newcome—Steam Engine, England
1734-1735	Peter Zenger libel trial and acquittal establishes freedom of press in U.S.
1750-1800	Scotland—Thresher
1756-1763	Seven Years War
1764	James Hargreaves—Spinning Jenny, England
1774	First Continental Congress in Philadelphia
1775-1782	Revolutionary War
1783	Jacques and Joseph Montgolfier—Balloon, France
1784	John Fitch operates steamboat on Delaware
1787-1807	John Fitch, Robert Fulton—Steamboat
1787-1810	Nicolas Appert—Canned food, France
1793	Eli Whitney—Cotton Gin, US
1796-1837	John Fitch, John Ericsson—Screw Propeller
1800	Henry Maudslay—Lathe, England
1804	Richard Trevithick—Steam Locomotive, England
1812-1814	War of 1812
1815	Humphry Davy—Safety Lamp, England
1815	John L. McAdam—Macadam Paving, England
1822-1839	Joseph Niepce, Louis Daguerre-Photography
1824	Joseph Aspdin—Portland Cement, England

WORLD EVENTS AND INVENTIONS (Continued)

1830	Edwin Budding—Lawn Mower, England
1834	Jacob Perkins—Gas Refrigeration, U.S.
1834	Cyrus H. McCormick, Reaper, U.S.
1835	Samuel Colt—revolver, U.S.
1837	John Deere—Steel Plow, U.S.
1839	Charles Goodyear—Vulcanized rubber, U.S.
1840	Sam Morse—Telegraph, U.S.
1842	Crawford W. Long—Ether, U.S.
1844	Gustave E. Pasch—Safety Match, Sweden
1844	First telegraph line laid
1845	Elias Howe—Sewing Machine, U.S.
1845	Robert Thomson—Pneumatic Tire, England
1846-1848	Mexican War
1850-1855	Ferdinand Carre—Ice making machine, France
1850	Edmund W. Quincy—Corn Picker, U.S.
1852	Henri Gifford—Dirigible Airship, French
1852	Harriet Beecher Stowe's Uncle Tom's Cabin published
1853	Elisha G. Otis—Safety Elevator, U.S.
1853	Charles Pravaz, Hypodermic needle, French
1853-1856	Crimean War
1855	Robert W. Bunsen—Bunsen Burner, Germany
1855	Henry Bessemer, Bessemer Converter, Great Britian
1855	First Atlantic cable laid
1857	Financial panic
1859	First petroleum well opened in U.S.
1860	Ernest Michaux—Bicycle with pedals, French
1860	Jean Lenoir—Gas Engine, French
1860-1870	Antonio Pacinotti (Italy) Zenobe T. Gramme (Belgium) Electric Generator
1861	Rene T.H. Laennec-Stethoscope, France
1862	Richard J. Gatling—Gatling Gun, U.S.
1861-1865	Civil War
1866	Seven Weeks War
1867	Christopher L. Sholes, Carlos Glidden—typewriter, U.S.
1867	Alfred Nobel—Dynamite, Sweden
1868	George Westinghouse—Air Brake, U.S.
1869	Isaiah and John W. Hyatt—Celluloid, U.S.
1869	Black Friday on Wall Street
1870-1871	Franco-Prussian War

1873	Joseph F. Glidden–Barbed Wire, U.S.
1876	Alexander Graham Bell, Telephone, U.S.
1876	Melville R. Bissell–Carpet Sweeper, U.S.
1877	Thomas A. Edison–Phonograph, U.S.
1877	Carl Gustaf de Laval–Mechanical Cream Separator, Sweden
1878	Anna Baldwin–Vacuum Milking Machine, U.S.
1879	Charles F. Brush–Arc Light, U.S.
1879	Thomas A. Edison–Incandescent Light, U.S.
1882	Henry W. Seely–Electric iron, U.S.
1882	Work on Panama Canal begun
1884	Lewis E. Waterman–Fountain Pen
1884-1930	Paul G. Nipkow, John L. Baird, Charles Francis Jenkins, etc.–Television
1884	Ottmar Mergenthaler–Linotype, U.S.
1885	Karl Benz and Gottlieb Daimier (German) Gasoline Automobile
1886	Hall, Heroult–Aluminum, France and U.S.
1889	Hiram Maxim–Machine Gun, England
1889-1896	Thomas A. Edison–Motion Pictures
1892	Whitcomb L. Judson–Zipper, U.S.
1893	Hugo Borchardt–Automatic Pistol, U.S.
1895	Gillette–Safety Razor, U.S.
1895	Wilhelm K. Roentgen–X Ray, Germany
1895-1902	Guglielmo Marconi, Reginald Fessenden–Radio
1897	Gold Rush to Alaska
1898	Spanish American War
1899	John Thurman–Vacuum cleaner, U.S.
1898	John P. Holland–Modern Submarine, U.S.
1899-1902	Boer War
1897	Diesel–Diesel Engine, Germany
1902	Willis H. Carrier–Air conditioning, U.S.
1903	Orville and Wilbur Wright, U.S.–Airplane
1903	Willem Einthoven–Electrocardiograph, Netherlands
1904	Digging of Panama Canal began
1904	Benjamin Holt–Tractor, U.S.
1904-1905	Russo-Japanese War
1904-1907	Fleming, De Forest–Radio Vacuum Tube
1906	Hermann Anschutz-Kampfe-Gyrocompass, German
1906	Pure Food and Drugs Act
1907	Louis and Jacques Breguet–Helicopter, France
1908	Jacques Brandenberger–Cellophane, Switzerland
1909	Leo H. Boekeland–Bakelite, U.S.

WORLD EVENTS AND INVENTIONS (Continued)

1910	Muck-raking era in American magazines
1914	Ernest D. Swinton—Tank—England
1914-1918	World War I
1922-1935	Taylor, Young—Radar
1923	Juan de la Cierva—Autogiro, Spain
1925	Birdseye—Frozen Food Process, U.S.
1926	Robert H. Goddar—Liquid Fuel Rocket, U.S.
1928	Drinker, Show—Iron Lung, U.S.
1930	Ernest O. Lawrence—Cyclotron, U.S.
1930	Frank Whittle—Jet Aircraft Engine, England
1930-1942	U.S. Companies, Mechanical Cotton Picker
1937-1945	Chinese-Japanese Wars
1939-1945	World War II
1939-1940	Russo—Finnish War
1940	Selective Service Act passed
1942	Enrico Fermi—Atomic Reactor, U.S.
1944	Howard Aiken—Automatic Digital Computer, U.S.
1945-present	Cold War
1947	U.S. Air Force—Supersonic Airplane
1947	Shockley, Bardeen, Brattain—Transistor, U.S.
1947	Edwin Land-Polaroid Camera, U.S.
1940-1953	Korean War
1953	John Gibbon Jr.—Heart-Lung Machine, U.S.
1954	Hyman Rickover—Atomic powered submarine
1954	Christopher Cackerell—hovercraft, England
1956	Bell Telephone Lab—Picturephone
1957-1973	Vietnam War
1958	Charles H. Townes, Laser, U.S.
1958-1963	J.F. Enders—Measles Vaccine
1963	Schoennakers—tape cassette, Netherlands

*Acknowledgement to *World Book Encyclopedias,* Field Enterprises Educational Corporation, Chicago, Illinois 60654 for some compiled information used in charts.)

PART II
PREPARING COMPARATIVE ARTS NOTEBOOK

After the student has selected a major figure from each of the lists presented, he is asked to make a notebook of not more than fifteen pages overviewing the artist's major contribution, background and the effect of the times upon this work. The student must be made to understand that quality of the workbook with introspective insight is more important than just the listing of titles of the artist's work. The goal should be to look at the artist as a byproduct of his time in history and the cause and effect of world events and inventions upon his work. The objective is to get the student to adopt a paternal attitude toward the listed artist and to seek an empathy with the figure. If the research is progressing properly, the figure should almost come alive and become part of the student's family, not just another paper figure in an art or music book.

Listings of books could be obtained from the librarian on art, literature, architecture, or sculpture. A supplemental bibliography list of such material could be a helpful aid to students as they research.

Often the most difficult aspect of this type of curriculum is to get the students to search for essential material. Another drawback is what would be considered a good outline for a handout sheet. A comparative arts guide question sheet is therefore presented along with three samples of detailed outline sheets for each specific year. The central artistic figure to be studied was Debussy. Encourage students to pick one specific favorite figure from all lists to elaborate upon.

STUDENT GUIDELINE AND QUESTION SHEET FOR COMPARATIVE ARTS COURSE

Part I.

A. Choose a person from each list correlating dates in history with the figure in; Architecture, Music, Painting, Sculpture, Literature and Invention. Note the effect world events had upon these figures. Inform instructor of your selection. Once selection is made, it cannot be changed.

Part II.

A. Research each figure in the school library. If extracting quoted material from books, footnote carefully. Place footnote sheet in back of the paper.

B. Choose one central figure from selection and follow through for his lifetime. Emphasize famous works by using records, slides or book quotations. Use opaque projector to emphasize book illustrations, postcards or other important samples.

C. Summarize paper by putting into your own words the effects world events, politicians, inventions, friends or family may have had upon the artist and his work. Think critically but fairly.

D. Paper is to be no more or less than fifteen pages not including title sheet.

Part III.

A. Present a ditto outline to all members of the class and teacher for the figures you have written about.

Be certain that all essential matter pertaining to your central artistic figure is contained briefly and carefully in the outline. A test will be formulated from this outline.

C. Prepare a fifteen minute illustrated lecture for class presentation from your notebook complete with samples of the artist work, background, or if a literary person is chosen, give a brief reading of his work emphasizing character, plot, time and a brief summation of the story.

TO AID IN PRESENTATION OF A GOOD NOTEBOOK
USE THE FOLLOWING QUESTIONS AS GUIDELINES:

1. Did wars impede or intensify the aesthetic work?
2. How did invention affect the times? The author, poet, composer, etc.
3. What significant action on the part of politicians caused the writer, composer or artist to alter his work?
4. Was there a war going on during the time anywhere in the world?
5. What was the financial and educational status of the artist?
6. Which significant friend encouraged the artistic work?
7. Did marital status play a part in the development of artistic work?
8. Did any type of scandal surround the artist's life?
9. Was the artist subjected to jealousy? By whom?
10. Whose music, literature, art work was the artist most influenced by?
11. What part did religion play on the artist, composer, sculptor's work?
12. What was the major contribution to history of this period?
13. What was the most important work of the artist, writer, composer to history?
14. What was the artist's favorite work?

COMPARATIVE ARTS
SAMPLE OUTLINE SHEETS

Sample 1: Emphasis on Literature

1868

WORLD EVENTS
President Johnson was impeached, tried and acquitted.
Grant was elected as the 18th president.
Professor A.E. Nordenskiold penetrated the pack of ice north of Spitsbergen to 82° -42'.
Sholes typewriter put into commercial use.

ART
Poverty drives Monet to suicide attempts.
Renoir lacks funds to buy paints—his "Lise" accepted by the jury and he is praised by the press.
Degas paints his first theatrical subject "Mlle Fiocre."

LITERATURE
Louisa May Alcott writes "Little Women."
A. Daudet, a naturalist, writes "The Little Thing"—often compared to "David Copperfield."
Paul Claudel, a French play writer, born.
Edmond Rostand, a French writer, born.
Francois Jammes, a French writer born—he was essentially a poet of the country side and of the beast of the field.
Stefan George, a German writer, born.

DEBUSSY
Nothing

GENERAL MUSIC
Brahms "German Requiem" completed.
Wagner's "Meistersingers" produced in Munich.
Sir Granville Bantock born.

Sample 2: Emphasis on Art

1881

WORLD EVENTS
Death of Disraeli—an English statesman.
President Garfield shot by a Republican fanatic.
Alexander the third—the ruler of Russia.
Louis Pasteur (1822-1895) applied the principle of immunization through vaccination of rabies.

ART
Sixth group exhibition, Monet ceases sending painting to the Salon entirely. Renoir travels in Italy, expresses discontent with Impressionist methods and is impressed by the Italian and antique painting classics. Cezanne paints with Pissarro and Gauguin at Pontoise, then retires to Aix-en-Province, his paintings emphasize structure and solidity, deny flimsy design and evanescent effects of Impressionistic work. Lautrec comes to Paris to study. Birth of Picasso at Malaga, Spain.

LITERATURE
Paul Verlaine—"Wisdom" one of the greatest books of religious verse in the world. Some of his best known works are "Moonlight" (Clair de Lune), "It Weeps In My Heart," "The Sky Is Over the Roof" and "Autumn Song."

A. Daudet, a French naturalist, writes "Numa Roumestau."
Henrik Ibsen writes "Ghosts."
Thomas Carlyle dies.

DEBUSSY

Debussy prepares for the Grand Prix de Rome. Meets Mme. Vasnier, the young wife of an architect, who is said to have been his mistress. Visit to Mme. Van Meck in Moscow in the summer. His compositions during this period were the following: Intermezzo for orchestra based on a passage from Hines Intermezzo, two songs Rondeau (Alfred de Mussets), Zephyr (Theodore de Banville).

GENERAL MUSIC

Brahms completes "Nanie," also the first performance of the "Academic Festival Overture," and the "Travic Overture."
E. Lalo writes "Rapsodie Novegienne."
Bela Bartok born.

Sample 3: Most Balanced Outline

1912

WORLD EVENTS

The steamship "Titanic" wrecked off the coast of Newfoundland.
Joseph Lister dies.
Wilson elected the twenty-eighth president.

ART

Delaunay, Picasso, Leger, Metzinger, Le Fauconnier exhibit with "Futurist" in Paris. Juan Gris joins the Villon brothers and Metzinger in the Section d"Or group and exhibits "Cubist" inspired painters with them.
Picasso and Braque begin to make collages. Picabia and Marcel Duchamp give their paintings exasperating far fetched titles, their forms become more mechanical in character as they make an effort to undermine formal purity in "Cubism." Kandinsky, Klee, Marc, Mache, and Munter form "Blue Rider" group in Munich and exhibit together.

LITERATURE

Paul Claudel, a French play writer, writes "The Tidings Brought to Mary," and "Agamemnon."
Arthur Schnitzler, an Austrian writer, writes "Professor Bernhardi."
Ricarda Huch, a German novelist, writes "The Great War in Germany."

DEBUSSY

Nizhinsky (22) produces for Diaghilev (40) a ballet on L'Aprismidi which meets with no approval from Debussy. He nevertheless consents to collaborate with Nizhinsky in Jeux. Begins the ballet Khamma for Maud Allan and entrusts its completion to Charles Koechlin. Compositions during this year are as follows: Chamber work "Syrinx" for unaccompanied flute, Ballet "Kbamma."

GENERAL MUSIC

P. Dukas writes a symphonic poem "La Peri."

A. Schoenberg's "Pierrot Lunaire" performed.

Vaughn Williams writes a choral work "Fantasy on Christmas Carols."

J. Carpenter writes "Chamber Music-Sonata."

C. Griffes writes "Tone Images," "Symphon in Yellow," "We'll to the Woods" and "Gather May" for voice and piano.

E. Whithorne writes "The Rain," an orchestral work.

L. Gruenberg writes "The Witch of Brocken" for theatre. He also writes his first violin sonata.

G. Bantock writes a choral work "Atlanta in Calydon" and an orchestral work "Fifine at the Fair."

Note: The above samples are high ideal outlines so that a student will demand a great deal of perfection by using these as guidelines. In no way should the instructor use these as average gifted student samples.

PART III
LECTURE WITH AUDIO, VISUAL SAMPLES

It is natural to culminate a course with a research paper or notebook submission, but in a comparative arts course for gifted students this doesn't force them to think on their feet. The students must be expected to understand the research they have carefully accumulated and be able to prepare an interesting lecture for fifteen minutes consisting of five minute overview of the times and figures they have studied. The next ten minutes they should explain the central figure for that period along with records of the composer, most famous works, slides or opaque projector material of background material, or the reading in brief of a famous writer's work. Rather than one fountainhead called music teacher, you have been replaced by many gifted lecturers each personally involved and responsible for their own assignment. The psychological implications of such an arrangement range from appreciation of the teachers efforts to prepare an interesting lecture, to a dedication to their particular art figure and his work.

There should be very little difficulty presenting slides, records, etc. if the music teacher refers back to the chapter of the Multi-Media Approach to Music Appreciation. A difficulty that may face music instructors is the availability of record samples of the composer's work. The music supervisor may use the following list as a guideline for ordering new records, or as a checklist for present recordings.

RECORD LISTS

The following record list takes into consideration these characteristics:

—Artists which best represent the composer's work.
—Records which are naturally seen in the university library list.
—Conductors that best interpret specific compositions.
—Fidelity and recording clarity.
—Allotment for individual preference.

NOTE: To decode the abbreviations given in the following list, use the most recent issue of the Schwann Stereo Record Guide. This guide can be purchased at any E.J. Korvette store in the country. (Headquarters: E.J. Korvette, Inc. 1180 6th Ave., New York, N.Y. 10009.

Medieval and Renaissance

Byrd, William: Mass in Four Parts; Westminster Abbey Choristers DGG ARC-198301

Des Prez, Josquin: Missa Ave Maria Stella; Hunster, U. Ill. Ch. Cho. L Motets None. 71216

Gabrieli, Giovanni: Canzoni for Brass Choirs; Chicago, Cleveland & Philadelphia Brass Ens. Col. MS-7209

Gregorian Chant: Benedictine Monks L-10-66 Phi. WS-9004

Lassus, Orlandus: Madrigals; Greenberg, N.Y. Pro Musica 4-11-65 Praetorius Dec. 79424

Medieval & Renaissance Music: Irish Harps, Viola, Recorders, Tambourine (11-65) Turn. 34019

Medieval Music & Songs of Troubadours Ev. 3270

Monteverdi, Claudio: Giani, Nuovo Madrigaletto Italiano (I) Lagrime: Lamento None. 71021

Palestrina, Giovanni: Choral Music; Missa Papae Marcelli, Theuring, Akademie Kammerchor West 9605

Praetorius, Michael: Canticum Trium Puerorum Terpsichore Collesium Schein: Widman DGG ARC-198166

The Baroque Era

Bach, Johann Sebastian: Brandenburg Concerti; Casals, Marlboro Fest. 2-Col. M 2S-731

Bach, J.S.: Concerto in D., 2 Violins S. 1043; Heifitz, Friedman, Sargent, New Sym. London LSC 2577

Goldberg Variations for Harpsichord, Landowska Vic. LM-1080

Jesu, Joy of Man's Desiring, Stokowski Orch. Sheep; Corelli: Con. Op. 6/8 Vivaldi Bach 70696

Mass in B; Stader, Topper, Haefliger, Engen, Munich Bach Orch. & Cho. 3-DGG ARC-270001

Passacaglia & Fugue in C for Organ; E.P. Biggs (hpsi) Bach Prog. Col MS-6804

Suites for Orchestra; Casals, Marlboro Fest. 2-Col. M2S-755

Toccata & Fugue in D for Organ, Biggs Col. MS-6261

Couperin, Francois: Concerts Royaux Harpsichord Music; Claude Jean Chiasson, Lyr. 12

Corelli, Arcangelo: Concerti Grossi, Op. 6, Phi. 900052

Handel: Messiah; Schwarzkopf, Hoffman, Phila. Orch. & Cho. 3-Ang. S-3657

Royal Fireworks Music, Appia, Vienna St. Op. Orch. Water Suite Van. S-209

Pergolesi, Giovanni Battista: Stabat Mater La Serva Padrona; Scotto, Bruscantini EV. S-445/1

Purcell, Henry: Dido & Aeneas; St. Anthony Singers (E) Oiseau 60047

Telemann, Georg Philipp: Suite in A for Flute & Strings; Rampal, A. Brott, McGill Ch. Orch. 7EV. 3194

Vivaldi, Concerti for Violin Van S-159

Vivaldi, Four Seasons, Stokowski, New Phil. Lon. 21015

Vivaldi, Antonio: Concerti for Violin: LaCetra Op. 9 3-Phi. PHS 3-993

Classicism

Beethoven, Ludwig Van

Concerti for Piano, No. 4 in G, Op. 58; Cliburn, Reiner, Chicago Sym. Vic. LSC-2680

Concerto for Violin in D for Violin, Op. 61; Oistrakh, Cluytens, Orch. Nat'l Fr. Ang. S-35780

Octet in Eb for Winds, No. 8 in C, Op. 59, No. 2; Rasumovsky, Janacek Qr. Parl. S-627

Quartets 7-16 (8, 14) Julliard Quartet Vic. LSC-2626

Sonatas for Violin & Piano (5, 9); Szeryng, Rubinstein Viv. LSC-2377

Symphonies No. 3 Eb. Op. 55; Barbirolli, BBC Sym. Ang. S-36461

Symphony No. 5, Dorati, London Sym. Mer. 90317
Symphony No. 6, Reiner, Chicago Sym. Vic. LSC-2614
Symphony No. 9. Reiner, Chicago Sym. 2-Vic. LSC-6096
Gluck, Christoph Willibald; Orfeo ed Euridice; Janowitz, Moser; Munich Bach Orch. & Cho. 2 DGG 2707033

Haydn, Franz Joseph
Concerto in Eb for Trumpet West. 14135
Quartets Op. 76, No. 3, Emperor DGG 138886
Symphony No. 45 Vienna Orch. Mus. Guild S-160
Symphony No. 88, Reiner, Chi. Sym. VICS-1366
Symphony No. 101 in D, Prague Sym. Parl. S-609

Mozart, Wolfgang Amadeus
Concerto for Clarinet in A. Kubelik, Berlin Phil., Leister DGG 136550
Concerti for Piano No. 20 Salzburg Mor. None. 71072
Don Giovanni, Danco, Dermota 4-Lon. 1401
Exsultate Jubilate, K. 165 Tel. S-43094
Overtures, Phil. Orch. Ang. S-36289
Quartets Nos. 1-4, Dover 5201
Requiem K. 626, Boston Sym. 2-Vic LSC-7030
Serenade "Eine Kleine Nachtmusik" LSC-2694
Symphony No. 38, Walter, Col. MS-6494
Symphony No. 41, Reiner, Chicago VICS-1366

Rossini, Gioacchino
Barber of Seville, Callas 3-Ang. S-3559
Weber, Carl Maria Von, Invitation to the Dance, Karajan, Ang. S-35614

Romanticism

Berlioz, Hector
Symphonie Fantastique, Bernstein Col. MS-6607
Bizet, Georges; Carmen, Callas 3-Ang. S-3650X

Brahms, Johannes
Concerto for Violin, Heifetz, Reiner 2-Vic. VCS-7058
Symphony No. 1, Ormandy, Col. MS-6067
Variations on a Theme by Haydn, Karajan DGG 138926
Chabrier, Emmanuel: Espana, Ormanda, Col. MS-6478

Chopin, Frederic
Grande Polonaise, Rubinstein 2-Vic. LSC 7037
Etudes, Horwitz, Col. MS-6541
Ballades, Horwitz, Vic. LM-1707

Mazurkas, Rubinstein, Vic. LM-2049
Nocturenes, Rubinstein, 2-Vic. LSC-7050
Preludes, Rubinstein, Vic. LM-1163
Waltzes, Brailowsky, Col. MS-6228

Debussy, Claude

La Mer, Reiner, Chicago Sym. Vic. LSC-2462

Prelude a L'Apres-Midi d'un Faune, Col. MS6271

Dukas, Paul, Sorcerer's Apprentice, Vic., VIC-1267
Dvorak, Antonin, Symphonies 7, 8, 9, Reiner, Vic, LSC-2214
Enesco, Georges, Roumanian Rhapsody, West. 14030
Franck, Cesar, Symphony in D, Boston, VICS 1034
Grieg, Edvard, Concerto for Piano, Cliburn LSC-3065
Peer Gynt Suites 1, 2, Boston, Vic. LM-2075
Liszt, Franz, Fiedler, Vic. LSC-2442

Mendelsohn, Felix

Midsummer Night's Dream, Ansermet, Lon. 6190
Mussorgsky, Modest, Night on Bald Mountain, Ev. 3053
Offenbach, Jacques, Gaite Parisienne, Col. MS-6546
Ponchielli, Amilcare, Dance of the Hours, Dis. S-4101B
Puccini, Giacomo, LaBoheme, Callas, 2-Ang. 3560
Rachmaninoff, Sergei: Concertos for Piano 2, 3 Cliburn Vic. LSC-2601
Rhapsody on a Theme of Paganini, Rubenstein LSC-2430

Ravel, Maurice

Rapsodie Espagnole, Stokowski, Sera. S-60104
Rimsky-Korsakov, Nikolai, Scheherazade, Reiner, LSC-24465

Schubert, Franz

Quartet No. 14 Death & the Maiden, Vienna Phil. Lon. 6384
Quintent in A, Trout, Serkin, Van 71145
Songs, Fischer, Dieskau, Ang. S-36342
Symphony No. 8, Casals, Col. MS-7262
Wanderer Fantasie, Rubenstein, Vic. LSC-2871
Schumann, Robert, Concerto For Piano, Cliburn, Vic. LSC-2455
Symphony No. 3, Solti, Vienna Phil. Lon. 6582
Strauss, Johann, Die Fledermaus, Waltzes, Vic. LSC-2500

Tchaikovsky, Peter Ilytch

Concerto No. 1 for Piano, Rubenstein, Vic. LSC 2681
Swan Lake, Ansermet, 2-Lon. 2204
Symphony No. 6, Monteux, Vic. Vics-1009

Verdi, Giuseppe; Aida, Callas, 3-Ang. 3525
Wagner, Richard: Overtures, Vic. LSC-3011
Siegfried, Idyll, Solti, 2 Lon. 2216

20TH CENTURY

Barber, Samuel; Adagio for Strings, Hanson, Mer. 90420
Bartok, Bela: Music for Strings, Percussion & Celesta, Reiner, Chicago Sym. Vic. LSC-2374
Britten, Benjamin; Young Person's Guide to the Orch. Bernstein 3 Col. D 3S-785
Copland, Aaron; Appalachian Spring, Dorati, Mer. 90246
Gershwin, George; Rhapsody in Blue, Ormandy, Co. CS-8641
Hindemith, Paul; Mathis der Maler; Col. MS-6562
Khachaturian, Aram; Gayne, Ballet: Suite, Vic. LSC-2267
Kodaly, Zoltan; Hary Janos: Suite; Dec. 9913
Mahler, Gustav; Songs of a Wayfarer; Ang. 35522
Mahler, Gustav; Symphony No. 2, Schwarzkopf, 2-Ang. S-3634
Mahler, Gustav; Symphony No. 4, Reiner, Vic. LSC-2364
Menotti, Gian Carlo; Amahl & the Night Visitors; Vic. LSC-2762
Milhaud, Darius; La Creation du Monde; Munch; Vic. LDS-2625
Poulenc, Francis; Concerto in G for Organ, Strings and Timpani; Ormandy, Col. MS-6398

Prokofiev, Serge

Classical Symphony; Bernstein; Col. MS-7159
Concertos for Piano No. 3, Cliburn; Vic. LSC-2507
Lieutenant Kije Suite; Ormandy; Col. MS-7528
Symphony No. 5; Oistrakh; Ang. S-40003
Schoenberg, Arnold: Five Pieces for Orchestra Mer. 90316
Schoenberg; Verklarte Nacht, Odys. 32160298
Shostakovich, Dmitri; Symphony No. 5; Previn; Vic. LSC-2866
Sibelius, Jean; Finlandia; DG 643212
Sibelius, Symphony No. 2; Lon. STS-15098
Strauss, Till Eulenspiegel; Bernstein; Col. MS-6225
Stravinsky, Igor; Firebird: Suite, Vic. LSC-3167
Stravinsky, Sacre du Printemps; Vic. LSC-3026
Villa-Lobos, Heitor; Bachianas Bachianas Brasileiras no. 5, Col. MS-6514

CHAPTER 8

Independent Guitar Study for Gifted Music Students

If we were to visit a large metropolitan zoo, the wolf pack would be fascinating visual study in behavior. The leader in the pack has head held high, tail upright and an aggressive mannerism. The followers appearance is much in reverse. The disturbing element is the sign out front of the zoological exhibition, "vanishing species."

The gifted student in a music program is very much like the leader of the wolf pack, head held high, delightful sense of humor and a natural sense of leadership ability. We must not make him feel as though he is a vanishing species. There is a great danger of labeling him "gifted" and isolating him from the pack of his peers. Sometimes this will cause students, especially the divergent thinkers, to vanish into their own projects at home and avoid programs designed for them. A built in safety guide was developed by using the gifted within the curriculum. The regular course goes on but the structure independent of the course is designed for the gifted specifically. In Music Appreciation it was the slide project and lists, in Music Theory it's more individual attention with more difficult tests or ear training exercises, in guitar it is extra lists and a flexible schedule which allows taking the guitar along with other students but at an accelerated pace.

Many high schools offer very popular guitar courses. What may surprise educators is that gifted students may not be enrolled in such a course. Attention was brought to enlighten this fact when a grand finale with full band accompaniment was being organized for a concert. A Spanish number was to be sung but the soloist needed a group of guitarists for accompaniment to add authenticity to the performance. To the music instructor's surprise the guitarists who offered to perform this task were gifted students that had not taken guitar when offered in the curriculum. When asked how they learned, they remarked, "We taught ourselves."

A truly experienced music instructor would not let an incident or comment drop with just a word of praise. Rather it would do well to investigate why such students slipped through the curriculum and yet chose to learn the guitar on their own. Do you know how many students in your music program have taught themselves guitar? Could it be possible that here lies another vein of creative giftedness that remains untapped?

With an awesome schedule of performance it is almost impossible to study every phase of gifted music students but it doesn't take much time to submit a questionnaire and tap this source of student information. Be certain to pass out the questionnaire during music periods. Do not allow students to take them home. Even well-meaning students lose or misplace these papers regardless of age. Have your music teachers ask the class how many students have taught themselves guitar. Suggest to these students that they bring their first guitar method book to class and their present favorite books the next day for class inspection.

The following day pass out the questionnaire to these students. Inform them that the music program is looking for new methods and answers to questions faced by a self-taught guitarist. The gifted student may then become a contributing figure to general curriculum. The music instructor will gain valuable insights as to why he chooses to teach himself or which books please a high school student. One must beware that some teacher-selected methods are very elementary and can cause an insult to older age levels.

QUESTION SHEET FOR SELF-TAUGHT GUITAR STUDENTS

1. What were the book titles, authors of the material you selected when teaching yourself how to play the guitar?

2. What was the most difficult obstacle you were faced with when learning the guitar?

3. Did any other student help you with learning guitar finger positions or chords?

4. What is the best way a school music program could have assisted you with your self-teaching guitar method?

5. Would you have preferred a course in school with an instructor rather than trying to teach yourself the guitar playing?

6. Rather than a course, would you have preferred a resource center which would contain slides, tapes, guitar books and the like to assist you in directing yourself to learning the guitar?

7. Presently, what is your favorite guitar book? Why?

8. Do you think a bibliography list of guitar method books would be helpful to you?

UNITING INTRODUCTION TO MUSIC WITH GUITAR

The questionnaire may cover the gifted student who teaches himself guitar. What is to be done with the gifted student who wishes to learn guitar, does not teach himself, nor is enrolled in a program? When a verbal survey was made of this, a consistent pattern structured around the "time" answer evolved. The gifted student often has many interests both creatively and academically. Naturally academic music will be chosen for credit over a guitar course because of college preparation. He may choose to skip a guitar course to have a shorter school day thus allowing time for an outside job. Basic guitar is simple and the gifted student often speculates that in-school time is too valuable to waste on some-thing as easy as guitar. Yet students consistently express a real desire to learn guitar. This places the music teacher in quite a dilemma. The natural answer is to just let the gifted student be. The guitar course is there if he chooses to avail himself of it. Although this is an easy answer to the problem, it is not the correct answer.

A more creative way to involve the gifted student into a popular program without relinquishing time and undue energy is to unite "Introduction to Music" with "Introduction to Guitar." The course will be general to all music students and is a forerunner to curriculum improvement in music. Gifted students will be drawn to the academic area of the course while general music students will find guitar performance an added incentive. Once the gifted student has learned basic chords, he can develop his own library of guitar books and go from there.

Some music purists may object to the combining of "Introduction to Music" with guitar but the results and practical advantages win over the argument. There is also an added advantage of injecting a guitar course into the curriculum with a minimum of disagreement from a budget minded school board. Ordinarily in a district, new courses demand the vote of school board members. By uniting these two courses into one, the guitar becomes an extension of an already existing course. Monetary compensations for the teacher become automatic since the same teacher teaches guitar and Introduction to Music.

Monetary need for the books, guitars, records etc. are automatically handled by the school budget allotment and can be supplemented by fund drives if the need arises.

The next question may be, How can one find a good academic teacher who can also teach guitar? Again the music industry comes to the rescue. Many guitar programs have been introduced within the past few years which have all but made the guitar a self-teaching instrument. The method books and group programs have been so numerous that it is almost a matter of judgment as to which one to choose. Our personal choice was *The Selmer Guitar Program, Box 310, Elkhart, Indiana, 46514.*

This comprehensive program involves all students including your gifted and relys on an AV teaching method. Since the instrument is easy to teach and learn, either in a group or singly, all types of music can be used to vary the extensive interest of the gifted student.

In a logical program sequence thirty-three lessons come on filmstrips accompanied by teacher's manual, student text and cassette tapes. It is flexible to handle any class size and can be taught by any teacher of music. The Selmer Company provides workshops for teachers to assist in presenting the program. The workshop format is similar to the regular program with the single variance of having only twelve lessons.

Each tape and filmstrip lasts about thirty minutes and can be stopped anytime for concentrated instruction. The amplifier has a special tuning feature and volume controls. Here again if some gifted students do not take the course, this program still provides two records or one cassette for students wishing to purchase these for self-teaching home use. The records·cost $5.95 and the cassettes $6.95.

This particular guitar program cost is a bit below others of comparable curriculum inclusion. Filmstrips, teacher's manual and "Combomatic" amplifier is $995. The Duquesene Filmstrip Projector is $167. Student correlated books cost $2.95 each. The Yamaha guitar made in Taiwan with classic nylon strings lists at $102 school price $65. A music company also will rent students guitars for a fee of $7 to $8 a month.

With a compact program in guitar, it is far easier for teachers to give personal attention to enrichment of the gifted by supplementing the course with a bibliography list of method books which will accelerate the student beyond the beginning stages.

SUPPLEMENTS TO TEACHING GUITAR

After the gifted student has availed himself of beginning techniques to playing guitar, a bibliography list of supplemental methods provide the student meaningful information with a minimum of time. Naturally space does not permit a listing of all the methods or books on the market today. Only your local music dealer can supply this information. However, do something a little unorthodox and include a list of the songs contained in the books. Gifted students always appreciate this effort because it saves time when ordering new books or when one goes into a music store to look through various guitar books. Any music teacher may extend the list by taking a tape recorder to the nearest music library dealer and recording new methods and songs on the tape. Later a listing can be made of this tape.

Each year the bibliography list should be updated to bring in the latest information. This listing can also serve other students in the guitar program if they are ready. All methods suggested frequently range from easy through intermediate to facilitate self-teaching as much as possible. Some of the books are good enough to be included in the guitar library. The instructor should take the time to review method books to suit the individual tastes which are as unique as teaching. Note that in the classical guitar section composers names are given more frequently rather than the selections named. This was done because classical selections are vague to many students.

Supplemental Materials List for Guitar

SELF-INSTRUCTION WITH CASSETTE

LEARNING UNLIMITED AUDIO-VISUAL GUITAR SERIES, (Book and Cassette $8.95) Windy, Green, Green Grass of Home, By The Time I Get To Phoenix, Games People Play, Everything is Beautiful

LEARNING UNLIMITED, 6525 West Bluemound Road, Milwaukee, Wis., 53213
(Level 1; Level 4 Country/Folk/Blues Guitar Course, Hal Leonard Publishing) Stand By Your Man, Make The World Go Away, King of the Road and others.

METHOD BOOKS

JERRY SILVERMAN GRADED GUITAR COURSE, Vol. 2 From Beginner to Intermediate (Keys G. F. D., 16th Notes, dotted eights and sixteenths, Chords in Key of ECF) Songs Arranged for Solo and Duet: The Wabash Cannonball, When the Saints Go Marching In, When the Moon Comes Over the Mountain, Ballad for Americans, Frankie and Johnny, Meet Me in St. Louis, High Noon, Over the Rainbow, Jeannine, The Riddle Song, The Foggy, Foggy Dew, Mairzy Doats, Chattanooga Choo Choo, Five Foot Two, Eyes of Blue, Whispering, Somewhere, My Love, JaDa, I'm the 47th All-Weather Man, Bill Bailey, The Gang That Sang Heart of my Heart, Peg O'My Heart, $2.50

BIG GUITAR BOOK $2.50 Carl Fischer, Inc. 62 Cooper Square, N.Y. 70
Big Note Arrangements by Leon Block
CATEGORICAL LISTING: I. Folk Music of Many Peoples; Brazil, Canada, English, Finland, French, Irish, Italian, Jewish, Mexican, Norwegian, Polish, Russian, Scottish, Spanish, Viennese

II. All Time Favorites such as: Stein Song from University of Maine, U.S. Air Force, Sweet and Low

III. Hymns and Spirituals; Adeste Fideles, Mighty Fortress is our God, Rock of Ages.

IV. Classic Selections; Chanson Triste-Tchaikovsky, Liberstraum-Liszt

V. Opera Selections; Musettas Waltz from La Boheme-Puccini or Toreador Song from Carmen-Bizet

VI. Children's Songs; Old King Cole, Now I Lay Me Down To Sleep

INSTANT FUN GUITAR, West Coast Publications, Inc. 4423 W. Jefferson Blvd. Los Angeles, Calif. 90016 $1.95 Alouette, Billy Boy, Blue Tail Fly, Buffalo Gals, Careless Love, Down In The Valley, Farmer In The Dell, Frankie and Johnny, Good Night Ladies, He's Got the Whole World In His Hands, Home On The Range, I've Been Working On The Railroad, John Brown's Body, Little Brown Jug, Long Long Ago, Mary Had a Little Lamb, Michael Row the Boat Ashore, Oh How He Lied, Oh My Darling Clementine, Old Grey Mare, Old McDonald Had a Farm, On Top of Old Smokey, Red River Valley, Row Row Row Your Boat, She'll Be Coming Round the Mountain, Silent Night, Skip To My Lou, There is a Tavern in the Town, This Old Man, Tom Dooley, Vive L Amour, When the Saints Go Marching In, Where Has My Little Dog Gone, Worried Man Blues, Yankee Doodle, Yellow Rose of Texas

EASY WAY TO GUITAR B, Mel Bay Publications, Kirkwood, Missouri 63122 $1.50 (Fine illustrations and organization) Good Bye Old Paint, Camptown Races, Long Long Ago, The Ash Grove, The Blue Tail Fly, The Gentle Maiden, The Waltzing Guitar, The Marines Song, Playtime, A Walk In the Woods, Drink To Me Only With Thine Eyes, Track Meet, The Blue Bells of Scotland, Sad Sack, The Up Stroke, Senorita, Dark Eyes, The Indian Maiden, She'll Be Coming Round the Mountain, Sleigh Ride, Hand Me Down My Walking Cane, In Old Spain, The Gauchos, The Sad Guitar, A Colonial Dance, Austrian Hymn, A Triple Play, March of the Giants.

THE NEW GUITAR COURSE by Alfred d'Auberge & Morton Manus Book 2, Alfred Music Co. Inc. Port Washington, N.Y. 11050 $1.95 (Must have teacher or student to help)
Oh How He Lied, The Horses Run Around, Double Notes Blues, Low Down Blues, Alma Mater, Beautiful Dreamer, Count Yourself In, Minka, Minka, La Cumparsita, (Solo or Duet) Our Boys Will Shine Tonight, Whose Gonna Shoe Your Pretty Little Foot, Four Ways to Turn, Six-Eight Rock (Student-Teacher Duet) Rakes of Mallow, The American Patrol, Lo-Hi Rock, Chicken Reel, (Sing and Play using alternating basses) I Know Where I'm Going, Careless Love, Midnight Sun, Devils Dream, Speed Drill, Battle of Jericho (Note: Magic Chord Accompaniment Guide in back for 3-D Rock, handy reference)

BOOGIE WOOGIE

THE GUITAR BOOGIE by John R. Griggs, Belwin Guitar Library, Rockville Centre, Long Island, N.Y. Level 2 (Pick Style)
Boogie Woogie Town, Spaceship, American, Spanish Canadian, Twilight Stoplight, Outer Space, Christmas, Gypsy, Flamenco, Brazilian, Satelite, Summertime, New York.

RELIGIOUS GUITAR

GUITAR SING-A-LONG FOR FUN AND FELLOWSHIP; Singspiration, Inc. Compiled by John W. Peterson Belwin Inc, Rockville Centre, LI, N.Y. 11571 $1.95
Along the Road, Amazing Grace, Bleeding Hands of Jesus, Burdens are Lifted At Calvary, For God So Loved the World, He Walked That Lonesome Road, Higher Hands, Holy Bible, Book Divine, How Beautiful Heaven Must Be, I Have Decided to Follow Jesus, I Know Who Holds Tomorrow, It Was Love, It's Not An Easy Road, Jesus and Me, Jesus, Wonderful Lord, Just a Wayward Lamb, Lord, I'm Coming Home, Mansion Over the Hilltop, My Father Planned It All, My Home Sweet Home, Only One Life, Over the Sunset Mountains, Precious Memories, Shepherd of Love, Softly And Tenderly, Sooner or Later, Springs of Living Water, Supper Time, Surely Goodness and Mercy, Thank You, Lord, The Haven of Rest, There Was No Other Way, This Is Why I Want To Go

SING-A-LONG FOLK

SONG FEST NO. 2400 SUPER SONG FEST, FOLK SONGS OF TODAY, Folk World Inc. 1860 Broadway, Ny. N.Y. 10023, (Old favorites with lyrics like Marching Through Georgia, Goober Peas, John Brown's Body to the less familiar The Dashing White Sergeant.)

EASY ARRANGEMENTS FOR GUITAR

EASY ARRANGEMENTS by Ernie Ball Guitar Special No. $2.95, Sloop John B, Cry Like a Baby, Young Girl, Summertime Blues, Hey Joe, (Viva Music Inc. Hollywood, Calif.)
EASY ARRANGEMENTS by Ernie Ball Guitar Special No. $3.95 Brother, Where Are You, Yellow Balloon, Sweet Inspiration, White Rabbit, St. James Infirmary.

SING-A-LONG-COLLEGE SONGS

COLLEGE SONGS, Charles Hansen Educational Music and Books, 1860 Broadway, New York, N.Y. 10023 75¢ (Sing-A-Long Book for lead guitar)

Across the Field, Carmen Ohio, Dear Old Nebraska U., Down the Line, Far Above Cayuga's Waters, Fight On, Go Northwestern Go, Hail Purdue, I'm a Jay Hawk, Indiana, Our Indiana, Iowa Corn Song, Men of Pennsylvania, Mighty Oregon, Minnesota Rouser, Navy Blue and Gold, Northwestern Push on Song, Notre Dame Victory March, On Wisconsin, Rambling Wreck from Georgia Tech, Sweetheart of Sigma Chi, Varsity, The Victors, Wave the Flag, We're Loyal To You Illinois, When the Irish Backs Go Marching By, The White Star of Sigma Nu

SLIDE & ELECTRIC GUITAR

SLIDE GUITAR by Green Note Publications Berkeley, California. (Book with record $4.95) Record guide to electric lead. and traditional slide and bottleneck stiles plus riff on open tunings. Special Chapters on improvising Blues and country. Musical examples are advanced and professional in nature but techniques can be learned by beginners.

BLUES IN E, COUNTRY SLIDIN, LOW DOWN D by Green Note Publications Berkeley, California. (Modern illustrations of contemporary men) Good for potential jobbing musician

SPANISH GUITAR

SPANISH GUITAR ALBUM arranged by Geoff Sisley, Boosey & Hawkes $1.25; I Know Where I'm Going, The Foggy Foggy Dew, I Have a Bonnet, I want To Go Home, The Star of the Country Down, My In Folk, The Lass of Richmond Hill, Charlie Is My Darling, The Girl I've Left Behind Me

BROADWAY HITS AND SOUL

BOX OFFICE BLOCKBUSTERS, Chappell & Co., Inc., N.Y., N.Y. $4.95 Broadway hits from My Fair Lady, Funny Girl, Finian's Rainbow, On a Clear Day, Bells are Ringing, Babes in Arms, Godspell, The Fantasticks, Paint Your Wagon, Pal Joey, Gypsy, The Boys from Syracuse.

SWEET SOUL MUSIC, West Coast Publications, Inc. 4321 West Jefferson Blvd. Los Angeles, Calif. 90016 $1.95.
Bring It On Home To Me, A Change Is Gonna Come, Land of 1000 Dances, Let's Go Get Stoned, A Lover's Question, She's Looking Good, Show Me, Since You've Been Gone, Stoned Soul Picnic, Sweet Soul Music, Think, You Send Me.

CLASSICAL GUITAR

CLASSIC GUITAR METHOD Book 2 Matteo Carcassi and Leon Block Alfred Publishing Co. $2.95
45 Classic Guitar Solos compiled by Alexander Shealy, $1.95, Lewis Music Publishing Co., 263 Veterans Blvd. Carlstadt. NY 07072 Composers: Bach,

Carcassi, Carulli, De Visee, Diabelli, Franck, Gaultier, Krakau, Marchetti, Newsidler, Polak, Ponce, Scarlatti, Sor, Susato, Tilman, Tarrega, Francisco, Valderraban, Zipoli

700 YEARS OF MUSIC FOR THE CLASSIC GUITAR Charles Hansen, 1860 Broadway, N.Y. N.Y. 10023 $1.95; John Dowland, Adam de La Halle, Johann S. Bach, Alessandro Scarlatti, Mauro Giuliani, Fernando Sor, Francisco Tarrega, Enrique Granados, Isaac Albeniz. (More advanced student)

MEL BAY VO. 1 CLASSIC GUITAR METHOD Kirkwood, Missouri 63122, $1.50, Little Minuet to Blue Tail Fly, Cradle Song by Brahms, Balkan Nights, The Little Prince by Mazas (easy)

CONTEMPORARY COUNTRY, FOLK, ROCK, BLUES

MAC DAVIS arranged by Howard Norman, Screen Gems-Columbia Publications 6744 N.E. 4th Ave. Miami, Fla. 33138 $3.50 (Piano, vocal, lyrics, guitar solos matching record album) $3.50
Beginning To Feel the Pain, Chop No Wood, Feel Like Crying, Lovin' You, Lovin Me, Sunshine, Way You Look Today, Woman Crying, Your Side of the Bed.

DONOVAN COSMIC WHEELS, Abkco Music Inc. N.Y. N.Y. Cosmic Wheels, Earth Sign Man, Sleep, Maria Magenta, Wild Witch Lady, The Music Makers, The Intergalactic Laxative, I Like You, Only the Blues, Appearances.

EASY GUITAR COUNTRY CLASSICS, The Big 3 Music Corporation 1350 Ave. of the Americas, N.Y. N.Y.; Gentle On My Mind, I've Got a Tiger By the Tail, Jackson, Knock Three Times, Green Green Grass of Home, Games People Play, Welfare Cadillac, The Wonders You Perform, That Lucky Old Sun, Make the World Go Away, El Paso, Long Lonesome Highway, Release Me, Suspicious Minds, You Don't Have To Say You Love Me, What's He doin In My World, Back in the Saddle Again, Cool Water, Heartbreak Hotel, I Almost Called Your Name, Just Walkin In The Rain, May You Always, Padre, Slow Poke, Taller Than Trees, The Wabash Cannonball, You Don't Know Me, Be Honest With Me, Crying In The Chapel, High Noon, I Walk The Line, In The Misty Moonlight, Mom and Dad Waltz, Tears On My Pillow, Wagon Wheels, Blue Suede Shoes, House of Blue Lights, I'm An Old Cowhand, Moonlight and Roses, Don't Let the Stars Get In Your Eyes, Walkin in the Sunshine, Bouquet of Roses

WORLDS GREATEST HITS OF CONTEMPORARY GUITAR by Charles Hansen Educational Music & Books, 1860 Broadway N.Y. N.Y. 10023 $4.95

SECTION ONE. POP-ROCK STYLES
Anticipation, Baby Blue, Bangla Desh to such songs as 25 or 6 To 4, You Can't Get There from Here.

SECTION TWO: COUNTRY-POP AND COUNTRYROCK

Act Naturally, A Boy Named Sue, The Happiest Girl in the Whole USA, Harper Valley PTA to other songs like Superman, The Year That Clayton Delaney Died

SECTION THREE: FOLK AND BLUES

All My Trials, Amazing Grace, Classical Gas, Joan of Arc to such songs as Country Roads, To Friends, Why I Sing the Blues

IMPROVISATIONAL GUITAR

ELEMENTARY IMPROVISATIONS FOR GUITAR by Ulf G. Ahslund Nils Aldeland, G. Schirmer, Inc. New York, $2.00

(Teaches how to improvise with guitar but must have the leadership of an able teacher and should be taught in groups.)

SELF-DIRECTED PROGRAMS
FOR GIFTED MUSIC STUDENTS

Self-directed programs must not be confused with self-directed curriculum like that used in the Comparative Arts Chapter. Rather the emphasis is placed on the convergent gifted performer who wishes to pursue music as a possible career or for immediate employment. Programs are set up to present the avenues which promote the least amount of difficulty. Each chapter is designed to structure the music teacher's goal of creating an excellent student teacher, one that will enrich not only feeder schools but present high school music programs. The gifted student will not be alienated from his fellow bandsman through special curriculum programs but basically structured to obtain necessary knowledge with a minimum of teacher direction in the everyday classroom situation. When the words "student teacher" are presented, often "college" is paralleled in thought. This needn't be the case. Many large high schools have produced superior musicians that teach younger students. Overcoming problems in a one-to-one confrontation early in a student's career sometimes teaches like no classroom curriculum can. Selection, control, teaching potential student teachers and obtaining necessary adult rapport will be discussed in detail.

CHAPTER 9

Choosing Student Teachers

Self-directed student programs can be very rewarding or very frustrating. To avoid problems, careful selection of a student teacher is mandatory. Emphasis will be centered on the instrumental music student.

How does one begin selecting a good student teacher? The first criteria is excellence in performance. A performer must have superior tone, technique, sight reading ability, rhythmic accuracy etc. Suggested technique for testing the above criteria are as follows:

SUPERIOR TONE QUALITY: Judge tone of all music people in the same room at the same time and in the same part of the room.

TECHNIQUE: Use exercise books or any material the instructor prefers that is idiomatic for that particular instrument. If technique is checked during rehearsal, the following ensemble books are recommended: *Unisonal Scales Chords & Rhythmic Studies for Bands by William C. White, Carl Fischer Inc. Ensemble Drill-Raymond C. Fussell, Schmitt, Hall, McCreary, 48 Pares Studies-Elmer P. Magnel, Belwin.*

RHYTHMIC ACCURACY & SIGHT READING: Test with *Watkins-Farnum Form A or B.* Use *Form A* if students have never taken this type of test previously. *Form B* is for students who have been tested by the Farnum test.

A daily check of tone quality, technique, rhythmic accuracy and blend can be accomplished through the following method:

Assign an ensemble exercise to the band, remind them that this exercise will be performed individually beginning with instruments which lend themself more readily to that particular assignment. Listen to each student individually but do not take more than 15% of class time daily. Continue this until all students have performed. Students not performing are requested to finger passages during performance of fellow students. All performances should be done with metronome to assure fluent technique. This procedure works best with smaller bands such as the divided band concept suggested previously. This allows for greater individual help on detail and is an aid to more accurate selection of student instructors.

USING CASSETTES

In every performance program there are students who fail to perform accurately because of extreme pressure created within themselves when they are asked to play before their peers. A student in this case should be allowed to tape these exposure exercises. Set up a tape recorder in one practice room and post a schedule for sign up outside the door. Have students announce their name and which exercise they are going to play.

This procedure could be done during the regular band rehearsal and must not be abused. Only one student at a time may be in the practice room recording. The music teacher must personally decide who psychologically is unable to perform well before the group. The above procedure also is helpful if a student had an excused absence during a particular section testing day.

The cassette method is also good if a particular student is having technique difficulties and wants to record progress over a period of months. Each month a tape may be made by that particular student and the instructor can take the tape home and evaluate progress from one period to the next. This substantiated information also serves as witness to performance grade if a student or parent objects during the grading period.

DO NOT use the cassette method in place of the exposure method. This was attempted for one complete year and the taped method created much less incentive and progress than the exposure method. Performing students need audience pressure.

SPECIFIC OVERVIEW OF STUDENT PREPAREDNESS

Ideally, every potential student instructor should have the following concepts well under control with precision and excellence:

Melody

1. Distinguish melodic variations (motive, phrase, sequence, theme).
2. Recognize common intervals.
3. Have an awareness of major and minor and pentatonic scale structures.
4. Develop singing approach to phrasing with instruments.
5. Experiment with interpretation of melody (dynamics, tempo).
6. Gain an understanding of how melody is used in various periods and styles.
7. Analyze score while instruments perform only main structural melodies (without accompaniment or conter-melodies).
8. Point out alterations in melody line (sequence, diminution).
9. Compare major and minor scales and tone row.
10. Continue developing playing by notation as well as by ear.

Rhythm

1. Strive for an awareness of rhythmic relationships.
2. Accurately reproduce all rhythmic patterns.
3. Count and clap rhythmic patterns.
4. Discover principal rhythmic motives which are used repeatedly in selections being rehearsed.
5. Discover, during rehearsal of a composition, parts to be played which serve primarily as a rhythmic function.
6. Stress independent maintenance of rhythmic patterns.
7. Strive for an awareness of complex rhythmic relationships.
8. Perform in unusual meters (5's and 7's. etc.).
9. Maintain rhythmic pattern against another rhythmic pattern.
10. Continue exploring parts which serve primarily as rhythm functions.

Harmony

1. Work for conscious harmonic intervals 3rds, 6ths, octaves).
2. Learn to relate one's own part to the total harmonic scheme by listening to it in relation to other parts.
3. Recognition of primary (I, IV, V) and secondary (II and VI) as performed.
4. Learn to recognize role played by certain notes of chords in creation of tension and release.
5. Recognize distinguishing harmonic characteristics of periods of music history as well as styles of musical composition.

Tone Color

1. Develop ability to recognize various tone colors through hearing them played by fellow students, teachers, etc. on various instruments.
2. Develop basic understanding of nature of sound and physical laws affecting rate of vibration.
3. Demonstrate effect of instrument with mute (when applicable).
4. Discussion centered around correct embouchure.
5. Study the vibrato as it relates to tone quality.
6. Special attention to unique parts of compositions which have been scored in a particular way for certain instruments.
7. Exchange parts to illustrate how some melodic styles are more suitable for one instrument than another.
8. Student has listened to a recording of an original version of a composition that has been transcribed for an ensemble or band.

Form

1. Has experienced an awareness of structure of rondo, theme and variations.
2. Recognizes repetition, contrast and variations in notation as an aid to score reading and memorizing melodies.
3. Has been exposed to polyphonic structure.

Expressive Skills

1. Senses the importance of tension, release and climax in a musical line.

2. Is aware that expressiveness may be attained through varying tone qualities, dynamics and tempo, vibrato etc.

3. Applies understanding of expressive values of rhythm, melodic and harmonic organization in playing.

4. Stresses interpretation of expressive markings, dynamics, tempo.

5. Knows the importance of not only interpreting expressive markings accurately, but also expresses beyond the markings to present a truly musical rendition.

6. Can perform a solo for band and takes constructive criticism well.

7. Plays under critical analysis for a judge at contest and can obtain a first division rating.

8. Is capable of performing before peer groups as unsigned criticisms are presented to the performer afterwards by this group.

9. Can perform in a group and as an individual at a moment's notice.
Example: Band performs difficult passage, first player plays difficult passage, band plays difficult passage again, gifted performer plays difficult passage solo.

10. Has tried to perform on an instrument other than his own (preferably instruments of the same family) thereby gaining versatility and insight into problems of performance.

Creativity

1. Experiments with melodic alterations, sequence, augmentation, diminution.

2. Explores possibilities of unusual metric groupings and complex rhythm patterns.

3. Explores possibilities of tone row.

4. Composes in a specific form.

5. Works for unity and variety in composition.

6. If student has taken harmony, should be expected to compose work for simplified piano score with basic chords inserted.

7. Can create simple arrangements for band such as (Happy Birthday).

8. Experiments with tape recorder. (Plays duets with self, records various sounds and puts them together.) Experiments with tape loops.

CHARACTER ANALYSIS

Aside from musical attributes, selection of a student-teacher on the basis of character, holds high priority. A student-teacher possessing good character and in harmony with the philosophy of the music department will, through his teaching, help to perpetuate qualities in the students he teaches. Essential character traits of integrity, enthusiasm, dedication, responsibility, compatibility, cooperation, citizenship, organizational ability, adaptability and compassion must be recognized.

Integrity

1. What is his attitude towards drugs, alcohol, sex and moral laws?
2. Can he be trusted to teach a very young student?
3. Is he honest with his school work?
4. Does he question moral hypocrisy at the adult and peer level?

Enthusiasm

1. Has a sense of joy and well being.
2. Knows himself and accepts success and failure.
3. Has a delightful sense of humor with the injection of small jokes or clever phrases for the enjoyment of all.
4. Has the ability to take a difficult task and overcome drawbacks without bitterness.
5. Can lose a personal contest gracefully and approach the next task with energy.

Dedication

1. Thinks of the group before personal gains.
2. Is willing to receive peer rejection in order that a long range goal is reached.
3. May disagree with director but extends suggestions for the common good.
4. Is willing to seek work over pleasure.

Responsibility

1. Offers to conduct a musical organization or volunteers to direct an academic project in class.

2. Can be chosen for spokesman.

3. Offers to do a task privately then organizes a group to assist.

4. May hold offices either in the musical organization or outside of it.

5. Excells in competition.

6. Keeps notes, library, instrument in top working condition.

7. Follows a given task to completion.

8. Notifies teacher of changes in working schedule or home responsibility then sees that proper certification is presented for verification.

Compatability, Cooperation, Citizenship

1. Punctuality in class and at performances.

2. Has the ability to get along with others.

3. Offers time to make an organization operate smoothly through library, paper work or instrument repair.

4. Is willing to compromise regarding the working student.

5. Can accept discipline when perfecting a difficult musical selection.

Organizational Ability

1. Is orderly about academic paperwork.

2. Promises to do something then sees that it is done (ie. props for half-time shows)

3. Remembers to take home instrument, clothing or personal possessions.

4. Does the amount of practice required and then some.

Adaptability

1. Doesn't react bitterly when disagreed with or asked to perform a task that is disliked.

2. Changes only the things that can be and accepts the decisions of the teacher when those decisions lie within the teachers responsibility.

3. Is willing to share social functions with others regardless of class standing, nationality or religion.

4. Is tolerant of others faults and doesn't try to judge or laugh at another's shortcoming.

5. Is objective about the student that may come late to a rehearsal.

Compassion

1. Takes time to assist a student with a difficult musical passage even though it is not required.

2. Will lend a sympathetic ear to a student with personal problems even though it is not a friend.

3. Will intercede in behalf of another student if teacher's decision seems unfair.

4. Is willing to extend time and effort to eliminate prejudice regardless of level by being an example of tolerance.

5. Replaces a negative comment made by a student with a positive statement for the condemned party.

The above concepts are obviously ideal and it is doubtful that any one student would possess all of the qualities enumerated. Each successive teacher will have to determine to what degree he will depart from the ideal and still find an acceptable standard to be applied in the selection of a student teacher.

CHAPTER 10

Controls for Gifted
Student Instructors

Self-Directed Learning with student instructors consists of student selection and evaluation of learning procedures, guidelines for organizing a student-administered environment and a set of carefully defined teacher behaviors.

The music teacher must determine the course objectives and goals in a Self-Directed Learning program. Each explanation and rationale can be described in one or two pages. These objectives should be presented to the student teacher before teaching begins, usually at the time of individual selection.

Student instructors are given the freedom to determine their own individual preferences for satisfying each of the goals through alternative choices. Alternatives should be written and handed to the music director for perusal. They are not permitted to decide with whom they will work but can determine when they will teach. Teaching is only permitted in the student's home under the indirect guidance of the parent.

Details related to the process of learning should be chosen by the student instructor. The learning plan consists of a written description of what the student intends to do, a diary of anticipated activities by day or week for each student, and evaluation procedure which can help determine the quality of work accomplished.

The final evaluation lies with the independent evaluation of a contest judge at the District and State Solo contests and the music director. If a particular student does not participate in contests, then the weight of decision lies completely with the music director for final judgment of student preparedness.

Once the student teacher's name is put on an approved list, he is free to direct his own teaching in these areas for a period of from one to two years. After this period of time, a professional teacher is recommended.

A significant part of the evaluation procedure is that it is so easy to control and very objective since an outside evaluator, such as the judge at a contest, determines progress. Students are expected to indicate:

1. A skill which results from proper teaching.

2. Be able to defend criteria upon which the skill was judged.

3. Determine how standards of quality are to be met in the future.

4. Expect positive feedback from the director of this student to determine if criteria and standards agree with him. No learning plan is approved without this evaluation procedure becoming detailed in writing.

ADMINISTRATION OF HOME-BOUND STUDENT INSTRUCTORS

An important element of Student Directed Learning concerns the roles assumed by the student teacher. Because most of the student teacher's time is spent on individual teaching of younger students and because the roles a music teacher can use are somewhat restricted, student instructors are expected to administer the record keeping, money collecting and disciplinary functions within the framework of his home. These might include keeping records of attendance and progress, organizing and maintaining sheet music libraries, theory books or establishing and enforcing disciplinary roles. The student, as an important individual then, is partially responsible for his own learning while the student teacher establishes proper environment with maximum elimination of phone, pets, young brothers and sisters or any other interference that may cause distraction from the appointed lesson.

Figure 4

**Gifted student teaching a young
drummer fundamentals of the instrument**

ROLE PLAYING OF THE STUDENT INSTRUCTOR

Which role will the student instructor choose to play?

1. Authoritarian

The student instructor is authoritarian in controlling and directing students to work within the lesson framework, maintaining the student-administered home and respecting the music director's roles. An authoritarian student instructor is one who lays the responsibility for keeping order and discipline within the students' group individually upon himself and does not expect any special assistance from the music director during the teaching period.

2. Explanatory

The student instructor explains the rationale behind the program—with relationship to his home—to the students. His or her limitations are explained to the music director. The student instructor understands why the music director uses certain techniques and accepts them, since it is that director a student instructor must please in the final analysis.

3. Questioning Specifics

During interviews, when a student instructor presents his learning plans for approval, what the band director says and does and how he reacts will determine the success or failure of the student instructor. The band director can ask for more details or examples or definitions of terms. Questions must be asked in a neutral non-critical tone that call for additional clarification.

4. Questions of Logic

Questions of logic call for clarifying relations, associations or connections. They may state unwritten assumptions or provide evidence and proof of statements.

What role a student instructor chooses to play will assist the music director in determining which manner he can and will be dealt with. Often much of the prescribed analysis can be handled quite easily since most directors have had student instructors a few years before assuming this position. However, written criteria assists in keeping the student instructor in hand and rests the real authority where it should be, in the hands of the music director.

Setting up goals and objectives is often the most boring part of curriculum. To avoid some of the apparent drawbacks, a curriculum rationale has been established so that the student instructor may use the following questions and fragmented statements as beginning points to establish proper goals. It is written in a progress report manner to allow flexibility of ideas and direct the student teachers thought patterns along the prearranged track of proper objectives.

STUDENT PROGRESS REPORT FOR STUDENT INSTRUCTORS

STUDENT'S NAME _____

STUDENT INSTRUCTOR'S NAME _____

STUDENT'S SCHOOL _____ STUDENT'S GRADE _____

DATE PRIVATE LESSONS BEGAN _____ TIME _____

(Fill out statements in brief sentences)

1. This student shows most progress in:

2. Student has most difficulty with:

3. I have assisted student with a special problem in music by:

4. Students general attitude is:

5. Student knows the major scales of:

6. Student knows the minor scales of:

7. Parents general attitude and comments are:

8. Student prepares private lessons with:

9. Student has most difficulty with the rhythmic patterns of:

10. I help the student with rhythmic difficulty through use of:

11. Student's attendance was:

12. I have given enrichment material in:

13. I plan to play duets next:

14. I have encouraged student to keep a scrapbook because:

15. I plan to hear this student perform at the following events: *(Circle at least one)* Winter Concert, Spring Concert, District Contest, State Contest

16. Judge your student on solo contest material as a judge would but instead of numbers write *Good, Fair or Poor*

INTONATION
TONE QUALITY
RHYTHMIC ACCURACY
FLUENCY OF TECHNIQUE
DYNAMIC CONTRAST
SENSITIVITY OF EXPRESSION

FEES

Even before establishing a student instructor program, the question of fees must be dealt with. When a program such as this was begun during the 1960's, student instructors received *$1.00* for a half hour lesson. Since, then, inflation has created a necessity for price changes. Setting uniform fees for all student instructors is mandatory if the program is to operate with a minimum of friction and envy. The director alone must establish student instructor fees commensurate with the economic stature of the area he serves. The fee must be low enough to allow the less economically capable to have their children study privately but must also be high enough to be worthwhile from the student instructor's point of view. There should, however, be a substantial difference between student instructors' and professional instructors' fees. A suggested fee for students is *$2.00* for a half hour with *$3.00* a half hour set for percussion instructors.

EVALUATION AND CONTINUANCE

The student instructor must be aware that although he will be basically teaching in his own home, there are certain rules which must be adhered to:

1. No beverages or smoking during lessons.
2. Interference kept to a minimum.
3. Complete attention to student and student's problems.
4. Demonstration of correct way to play a note. Insist the student play after instructor, correcting deficiency immediately.
5. No phone interruptions or pets distracting.
6. Television and radio must not be on during lessons.
7. Establish a sense of humor, make the student feel at ease.
8. Correct with kindness.
9. Avoid shouting or losing temper. Be firm but fair.
10. Make the student feel as if he or she is the most important person in the world.

Although the above statements should have been handled by the student instructor with just plain common sense, it is amazing how many instructors have been abusive to such easy rules. Often the director judges on his own maturity rather than the student instructor's level and simple rules never reach the instructor because of this innocent failing.

CONTINUANCE OF STUDENT INSTRUCTOR

What criteria should a music director use in determining dismissal of a student instructor? The band or orchestra director at the elementary and Junior High level should exert the greatest amount of authority over the high school student instructor as it is the elementary students who will be most affected by the student instructors. Also, it is at the elementary level that the director studies the potential student instructor. For an effective program, it is imperative that the High School music director have excellent rapport with the Junior High and elementary directors. Often just a verbal conversation with a Junior High Director when reviewing potential candidates or continuing student instructors leads one in appropriate directions. Three areas need constantly be reviewed: student teacher attitude, skillful teaching results, enjoyment in teaching.

Often even the Junior High or High School teacher cannot evaluate the student instructor. Past experience recalls an exceptionally talented girl cleaning her desk drawers while teaching. Another, a boy, reading a book and doing homework while teaching. Even the best can get sidetracked and must be corrected. That is why constant student and parent feedback is necessary. If you hear by word of mouth anything of this nature see to it that it is corrected immediately. Get on the phone and check things out frequently. Attitudes such as those mentioned cannot be accepted.

Beware of prejudice. Blacks prefer black student instructors and even though a white teacher may say it is all right to have a black student come to the house, his neighbors may object. Be honest with students and expect them to be honest with you. Seek minimum control but do control.

CONTINUANCE OF IMPROVEMENT IN A STUDENT INSTRUCTOR

While a student instructor is teaching in a home, it is of utmost importance that he or she continue instruction from a professional private teacher on their particular instrument. In this manner, should a need arise as to correct emboucher, particular fingering, or exposure to new literature, the private professional teacher is on hand to answer pertinent questions. This allows the individual music director to operate independently of the student instructor in another facet of teaching. If a high school student refuses to abide by this request then he or she should be dropped from the register.

In the past both the private teacher taking lessons and those who stopped taking lessons after the sophomore year were compared for student performance. The student continuing lessons displayed definite positive results when it came to their own students' performance rating at a contest. It might be suggested that the self-improvement technique enhanced private teaching through positive feedback.

A private lesson exception can be made in the Senior student teacher. At this stage, concentration on college or possible continuance in music at a professional level proved enough incentive to be reflected in student instructor performance. However, the music director should pass final judgment in this area since each student is unique and each responds differently to responsibility.

CHAPTER 11

Placing Student Instructors

Articulation between Junior High and High School is absolutely essential to the growth of a strong and healthy student instructor program. Even before developing a teaching register there must be a two-way communication developed between Junior and Senior High music directors. Many high schools have attempted to develop such a rapport by establishing teacher institute and teacher workshops. In this capacity, it is interesting to observe that the most frequent request by Junior High teachers was for more communication. From this can stem breakfast meetings, workshops with round table discussions, or personal invitations to concerts. If this type of communication has not been developed in a particular school system then a questionnaire may aid in obtaining pertinent information.

FEEDER SCHOOL QUESTIONNAIRE

1. Names of full-time Band, Choral or Orchestra Directors:

2. Names of part-time staff:

3. Names of Private Instructors:

4. What is the purpose of your Beginning band, choir or orchestra?

5. Where do you place emphasis in Cadet Band or Orchestra, Middle Choir?

6. What are the goals and objectives of your Symphonic Band, Orchestra, Madrigals, Senior Choir?

7. Do you have a Jazz Band, improvisational orchestra group or improvisational choir? Why?

8. What is the calendar of your events?

9. What would you like to see the instrumental or choir teachers do at the High School?

10. How can better articulation be developed?

Although the questions were brief, the answers revealed a good deal about the feeder school director. After visiting a rehearsal or two at the feeder school the High School director was in a better position to assist Junior High School directors when the need arose. Perhaps the most enlightenment came from the answers to questions nine and ten. A brief summation is listed below:

WHAT WOULD YOU LIKE TO SEE THE INSTRUMENTAL TEACHERS DO AT THE HIGH SCHOOL?

1. Academic achievement to music education with emphasis on training all students for a professional occupation.

2. Participation in the District and State Solo and Band contests for proper evaluation by peer educators and for proper tangible achievement of students.

3. More individual emphasis on concept of good tone and projection. Exposure to various styles of music such as the Romantic, Classical and Contemporary periods.

4. Advancement from Junior Varsity band to Concert band on musical achievement not age.

5. Wider expanse of musical advancement between incoming freshman and High School Juniors and Seniors.

6. Performance of finer band literature i.e.:

Finale from Symphony No. 3 by Giannini
Ein Heldenleben—R. Strauss
Il Re Pastore Overture—Mozart
The Roman Carnival Overture—Berlioz
Scenes from the Christmas Pantomine "The Miracle" by Humperdinek
   arr. by Bainum
Concerto in D Flat for Two Trumpets &, Band—Vivaldi
Overture for Band—Mendelssohn
Prolog to the Opera "Mefistofele"—Boito

7. A group of fine professional private instructors to encourage High School students to continue professional private training.

8. To hear the High School Band accompany an outstanding national soloist and receive exposure to an artist clinic which the soloists give.

9. Musical testing to improve performance of scales and evaluation by such music tests as Watkins-Farnum.

10. Development of prideful achievement of the band through competition with other schools.

11. Training musicians for a career in music and for college.

12. Training musicians for immediate job opportunities by qualifying for the American Federation of Musicians exams.

HOW CAN BETTER ARTICULATION BE DEVELOPED

1. Private instructors in High School with continued training from professional instructors be used as teachers for grade school.

2. Classical advanced concept of music literature so that High School student can be used as a symbol of proper breath support, beautiful tone, rhythmic accuracy in a clinic capacity for the younger student.

3. Better concept of Music Theory so that the High School student can teach correct principles to the grade student, simply but effectively. Perhaps even have his student play a simple melody he has composed in a theory class.

4. An outstanding High School Band whose honors could be looked up to by the grade school, whether at a concert, on T.V., at a football game half-time show or at a parade, is always added incentive.

5. Performance of band literature that Grade school musicians would be unable to perform.

6. Music training which would train talent for anticipation of professional performer, thus exposing young students with tangible proper *"hero worship."*

Under articulation we can clearly see that the student instructor holds an important key position to communication not only from the music director's point of view but from the student being taught by a High School student instructor. There is no question that using high school students and private teachers will improve a feeder school. This has been proven over and over again. Here again we see proof of its significance and importance. Using student instructors and applying questionnaire information, assist the music director in establishing a consistent campaign to register the best private teachers and use them immediately.

After guidelines are established for the private instructor along with goals and objectives fee and philosophy, communication between Junior High and Senior High music directors must be cemented. When this has been accomplished begin to write up a list of private instructors under the following titles:

NAME   ADDRESS   PHONE   INSTRUMENT

List names according to instrument groups. Obtain a line map of each city for available quick reference by secretaries. Usually such maps are available on the inside of telephone books for the local area. Have a student draw the map on a large poster board.

CHARTING A TOWN

Choose a secretary who is familiar with the streets in a town. After the charts have been duplicated on poster board, the secretary should review the register list of private instructors and note where they live. This needn't be marked on the chart, just as long as the secretary is familiar with the street. The purpose of familiarity is of assistance when a parent approaches the secretary signing up for private lessons. The secretary will suggest the private instructor closest in address or location for the new student and thereby eliminating missed lessons due to transportation problems. Be certain that the secretary set up her booth on the same day that band recruitment is going on for new instruments. Both professional and student instructor's lists should be on hand. The parent should be asked, "Which would you prefer a professional or student instructor?" Know the fees and discuss the advantage of a professional instructor. It isn't necessary to sell the private student instructor most, parents prefer making minimum expenditures of money in lessons until they are certain the student will continue with the instrument.

PROBLEMS AND HANDLING PROCEDURES

There is no ideal teaching situation as there is no ideal teacher. A student instructor, no matter how high the ideals, may find boredom entering into the teaching picture. Maturity can help to recognize and adjust to problems. This is not so with student instructors as they do not have that maturity. Teaching doesn't have the aura it once had but the student teacher doesn't want to give up something he finds very lucrative. Boredom will show up in the student instructor with the following signs: omission of attendance at a concert or contest, not paying attention to the student during a private lesson, giving a twenty minute or less lesson instead of the 30 minute requirement.

Lack of responsibility is the next sign. Student instructor will have excuses for not obtaining necessary contest literature for solo contest. Loss of temper often occurs when a High School student finds it difficult to get teaching principles across to a younger student. Loss of the temper is not as bad as HOW a temper is lost. Throwing any object either around the room or at the student is highly objectionable but it is a possibility.

Gossip can cause many problems especially when a student instructor discusses the progress of a particular student with another high school student instructor. A student may seem mentally slow but the word *"stupid"* is as lethal to any music program as the word *"win"* is essential to an athletic contest. Using the phone while teaching is just as forbidden.

Four dollars an hour is a nice sum of money but the face of greed soon crops up when a gas station attendant shows his long extra hours with a payment of a new roll of bills. Even though this roll may be dollars the high school instructor is tempted to raise his fee. Prudence guarding this weakness must result in holding the money line and the individual music director must do it.

Lack of interest will sooner o later crop up in many instructors' lives. Often an impending college expense promotes desire for a more secure paying sales position. The student instructor should not be permitted to transfer his students to another student instructor. The music director decides the transfer procedure.

With the exception of the last comment, handling of these apparent deficiencies is done on the *"three strike"* principle: first a warning, second a conference with the music director, third dismissal.

PARENTAL AND STUDENT FEEDBACK

The impression received after presenting various negative aspects of teaching is that in all cases the student instructor was at fault. Clarification should be made that in some cases personality conflicts may give the appearance of lack of interest on the part of the student instructor. Here we must rely on conferences and talks with parents of the students taking lessons. Encourage parents to talk about their child's progress after band rehearsals. Ask how well the student is getting along with their private instructor. Get to know the parents so that you can determine a vindictive statement from a real complaint. Make it a point to send home progress reports. In High School this may take the form of supplementaries. In the Junior High encourage your feeder schools to do the same thing. They need only take the supplementary as guidelines and adjust statements to a simple card.

Be certain to make the telephone your major source of communication. It is preferable for you to call the parents just to say you enjoy their child in band or that you are not getting the work out of their son or daughter to which they are capable. The time spent on this personal touch reaps rewards that no Band Parent Organization can compare. Talk to fathers, when calling, if a particular student is rebellious. Doing this often saves the student instructor hours of defensive statements. Letters or small notes are a must for a busy schedule. Suggest to parents that they use this form of communication whenever a problem or suggestion for improvement may arise.

The student instructor should feel free to come into any band rehearsal, notifying the director that he would like to discuss a private matter after the rehearsal. Not only will the instructor gain from observing a band in progress but will be trained to realize that the director's time is limited. To this day even when student instructors are off to college, notes frequently proceed their visit to a rehearsal and discussion about their students.

Obtaining proper feedback is a matter of training whether it be a parent or instructor. Limit always to three forms: telephone, letter or conference. Use these forms even when student disciplinary procedure must follow. Students should know what is expected and that there is a certain amount of compassion required of a teacher.

Research again reveals that a student will imitate the teacher he has had in school. If you are the teacher, then the student instructor should be excellent and few disciplinary procedures will be required. Remember these student instructors are a highly select group and should be treated accordingly. The voice should never reach above a medium level. Firmness with fairness should be the rule. Often they are aware that they have done something wrong and will be defensive to the point of lying. Realize that this is a face saving device and weigh carefully. A music director in this case will have to be judge and jury. If help is needed, rely on the comments made by the professional private teacher about his student, the student-instructor. No one need be alone in these decisions.

Realize that your position is as judge of the independent study and that 90% will depend on leaving decisions in the hands of the student instructor. Only in cases of negligence must your 10% be enough to dismiss a student.

Feedback whether from student, student instructor or parent should be the thermometer of a good student instructor teaching program; then discipline will be at the very minimum.

CHAPTER 12

Teaching Gifted Students to Test and Tune Individual Instruments

Before attempting to teach your gifted students to tune individual instruments in the band it is wise to review each instrument and its intonation variances. In this manner, a player will know which notes on his particular instrument have a tendency to be out of tune and whether the tendency is sharp or flat. One of the best ways we have found to determine this is to write out a chromatic scale for the complete range of each instrument, then provide duplicate notes where there are several fingerings available. By tuning the instrument to a well tuned organ or piano or by using a Stroboconn, the student can match his notes to the equal-tempered scale of the instrument employed and mark with arrows the notes which are out of tune with this scale. The arrows should point up if the note is sharp and down if flat. Longer arrows or some other device can be used to mark the notes which are further off. The knowledge gained from this type of marked chromatic scale must be used in conjunction with listening while playing, because playing in tune requires ALL players to match each other. This can be done only by listening and humoring tones. It is wise to have each player keep this chromatic scale of instrument variables in his music folder so that the gifted student tuning his section can refer to it in the beginning training period of tuning a section.

Just as an instrument maker tests new instruments to see what they can and cannot do, so too can the music student test his instrument. Duplicating the chart on the next page and giving it to your students will aid in understanding of the technical physics of an instrument. The gifted student can then ask the performer what notes on his particular instrument have little response and learn to adjust accordingly.

Our primary concern is to develop a gifted student to have sufficient ear training concepts before teaching him to tune a band instrument. Now that the director has sufficiently analyzed instruments in his organization by using the prior method, training the gifted students on individual tuning can begin. It is advisable that your gifted players have had Music Theory and ear-training before attempting to build knowledge of individual instruments. In this chapter we have designed a series of procedures for tuning each instrument section in a band. Rather than tune each instrument individually by the band director, use your gifted students that showed especially talented *"ears"* in a previous theory class or ear-training tests.

We shall begin by giving specific instruction for tuning each instrument and the care and maintenance of each. Take this information and have it duplicated as handouts for each gifted student or you may wish to use the complete compiled information in a "Student Handbook," to be given to all students as visual aids in the complex task of tuning.

It is helpful after presenting the material to demonstrate by tuning each section. In the process of tuning, have your gifted leader take notes on just what you are doing in that particular section. This will help as a memory refresher when notes can be coupled with the handbook. The gifted leader may ask questions as you go along.

WARNING: DON'T TUNE THE ENTIRE BAND IN ONE SESSION, RATHER TAKE ONE SECTION AT A TIME IN EACH REHEARSAL.

This procedure works well for training individuals to make each section responsible for tuning as a daily procedure. It also releases the director to tune the entire ensemble and spend less time on individual sections in later rehearsals.

Notes for Testing Wind Instruments

(All notation indicates written pitches for the instrument)

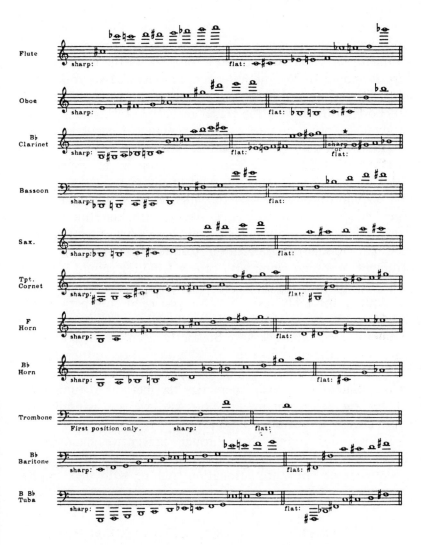

*Depending on the strength of the embouchure—weak-flat; strong-sharp.

3.

The Technology of Making and Maintaining Instruments

There is a negative side effect to this procedure of tuning sections:

1. Students in the section rely on the director's ear for correcting instrument intonation variables.

2. Students rely on the gifted leaders to correct tuning variables.

In order to eliminate dependency on the director, we have found that establishing a habit of having each person check his instrument for pitch with a Stroboconn places the responsibility where it should be, on the individual musician. Have your gifted leaders ask the student if he has checked his instrument with the Stroboconn before having the leader recheck for intonation. Make it a standard procedure to use the tuning bar, Stroboconn, or Strobotuner naturally daily. Another procedure is to have your gifted leader stand to the right of the tuning equipment and recheck each student making fine adjustments.

We cannot stress too much the importance of cleanliness and proper handling of instruments. Along with the tuning of a particular instrument, all leaders should have a list of trouble areas which are normally neglected in maintenance and care of an instrument. Warnings along with proper handling should be a part of all intonation instruction. When the leaders are trained to do these tasks responsibly, as a director you need only periodically check or handle the student that is continually negligent.

You will notice that we have obviously given the procedure for tuning a specific instrument in *"capsule"* form rather than a lengthy technical approach. We have found that this procedure gets the student to quickly memorize the method of tuning and then the ear is used more quickly. Also we are assuming the student already knows how to tune.

We have also found that through preventive maintenance coupled with tuning instruction less instruments are in repair and thus allow more time for intonation training with that specific instrument.

TUNING CORNETS, BARITONES, BASSES AND SINGLE HORNS

Many brass intonation problems are caused by dents. Generally dents closer to the mouthpiece have a more adverse affect on tuning. Double and triple brass plate at the lead in pipe help to insure the correct dimensions at this vital area. Most brass players concede that the first eight inches of tubing are the most critical regarding tuning and tone quality. If there are dents anywhere within eight inches of the mouthpiece of brass instruments in your section notify your director immediately.

Under most conditions, no brass instrument should be played with the tuning slide completely in, as this causes extreme sharpness. Tuning to one note and drawing the tuning slide to render the instrument in tune does not guarantee an in-tune brass instrument. Most players concede that when the tuning slide is drawn out too far (as tuning to a flat piano) it then becomes necessary to draw the 2nd valve slide out a given length, the 1st valve slide out twice that length and the 3rd valve slide three times that length. It is extremely important that the 3rd valve equal the first and second. Low C# and D must be compensated with the slide provided. This is especially necessary on long tones.

Trouble Shooting Maintenance

1. Check to see mouthpieces are washed at least once every month.

2. Look for dents in the lead in pipe eight inches from mouthpiece.

3. See that all slides work smoothly and are lubricated properly.

4. Check for loose pads.

5. Frequently overlooked on the Trombone is the cleaning of the cork barrels. Check these.

TUNING THE BASSOON

The embouchure of a good bassoonist should be relaxed and round. An approximation of a good embouchure can be obtained by making an "OO" as in "dew" sound without changing the lips, then an "ah" sound. Result is the lowering of the jaw. Cover the teeth with lips very thinly but not like the oboe embouchure which allows no pink of lips to show. NEVER USE A SMILE EMBOUCHURE.

Reeds

The importance of good reeds cannot be emphasized enough. Often it will be necessary to adjust the reed slightly to suit individual needs. This can be done with a small flat file, knife, sandpaper, and a pair of pliers. The reed should be graduated in thickness from back to front with thickest part in back. It should also be graduated in thickness from side to side. Have the sides thin and center thick.

If reed is flat, cut a very little of the end of the reed about a 32nd. BE VERY CAREFUL, this practice can affect the reed quite easily.

If no response in low register, reduce reed at very back, more at sides than in the center.

If reed does not speak on particular notes, file the very tip.

If reed sounds thick or muddy, open by pinching second wire.

If reed is closed, open by pinching first wire.

Care and Maintenance of Bassoon

1. The crook or bocal is more apt to become dirty than any other part. Clean with a small brush on a wire regularly or use a pipe cleaner.

2. The tiny pin hole in the crook must be kept clean. A pin or needle can be used but must not enlarge the size of the hole. CAUTION.

3. The wing needs several types of care. After playing, dry out with a cloth. Do several times to absorb all moisture. Make sure the cloth is small enough to go through even the smallest part of the wing.

4. The holes should be cleared by blowing through each before swabbing.

5. Flick keys should be removed and holes cleaned at least once every six months.

6. The crook is made of very soft metal so grasp firmly but never force into instrument. When taking instrument apart always remove the crook first making sure that the whisper key is depressed.

7. Take the bell off next, the long piece, wing. The long piece and wing are dismantled separately.

8. Keep away from heat.

TUNING THE CLARINET

Because woodwinds generally cause greater tuning problems than brasses, it is important to remember that tuning this section requires extra care. One effective means of tuning the clarinet is to use a Bb tuning bar and tune the open G (an interval of a fourth). Next tune high C (concert Bb). All of the above tuning is accomplished by adjusting the barrel. Use tuning rings if necessary.

The next step would be to tune middle C (Concert Bb). At this point adjust only the middle joint of the instrument. Assuming that the clarinet is acceptable quality, the tuning of remaining notes is in the hands of the performer.

Preventive Maintenance of the Clarinet

1. Swab after every playing session. A handkerchief is the most absorbent swab.

2. Especially common is accumulated dirt and grime in the tone holes. Make sure the register hole and tone holes have not been accumulating dirt, clean with pipe cleaner.

3. Dryness is the most common cause of loose or frayed tenon corks, use cork grease.

4. Watch pads over closed holes when cleaning and applying bore oil. Oil will cause skins of pads to dry and harden which will cause the pads to leak.

5. Three out of four clarinets have mouthpieces that must be acid cleaned to remove the accumulated deposits caused by improper cleaning. The resonating chamber of a woodwind mouthpiece is as sensitive as the resonating chamber on a violin so keep free of obstruction. Check mouthpiece for cleanliness at least every two weeks.

6. See that clarinets in your section are never laid on their keys.

7. See that a reed cap is always placed over the clarinet.

8. See that everyone in your section has two good reeds.

9. Suggest to your section that clarinet cases be left open after practicing at home to help dry out the instrument. Suggest that a piece of camphor be placed in the case during the summer months when the humidity is high. This will absorb moisture when the case is closed.

10. See that clarinets are not placed near radiators, hot air registers, or stored in hot attics. Neglect such as this results in cracked clarinets.

Tuning the Drums

Make sure the sound is the same at each rod of drum by truing head. Tap two to three inches from rim and adjust tension with the drum key. Be very careful and take plenty of time because the turn on one rod affects pitch directly opposite. Upon completion of truing head put pressure in drum's center, seat and remove any slack. Recheck tone at each rod again. The in-tune head should vibrate evenly and produce a clear tone. It is wise to see if the same number of threads are showing on the lugs.

Tuning Snare Drums

1. Tense at mid-range and see that the center of head can be indented to no more than half an inch. Pitch heads a minor third or interval of a major second.

Bass Drum

1. Bass will resonate well if back head has been tuned slightly higher than batter head. Remove slack by applying pressure to head center with hands or knee. This drum should have an in-depth long resonant sound if properly tuned.

Timpani

This instrument must be tuned most carefully. If there are any squeaks, check lubrication of rim.
Put pedal in position UP then:

1. Tune D below bass clef on 30" drum
2. F on 28" drum
3. Bb on the 25" drum
4. Tune D an octave above the 30" drum upon the 23" drum.
5. Now remove foot and put in the mid range position, true.
6. Move to down position pitch sound should be a fifth above low note, true again. If using a set of four drums tune C major chord (GCEG), and make pitch adjustment around drum.
7. When not in use, Timpani pedal should be in DOWN position in tune to the upper range until head stretches and is seated.

Bongos, Conga and Timbales

1. Tune Bongos HIGH. The bigger bongo should sound a fourth lower than the smaller one.
2. Tune Conga to Middle C on the 11 inch drum.
3. Tension timbales to middle range. Thumb pressure should indent timbale no more than half an inch.

Drum Sets

Most jazz drummers like a resonant sound which is very clear in tone. To obtain this quality:

1. Tom-tom pitch should have tone of triad in the root position from the floor tom UP. Two drum set has tom-tom pitch of fourth or fifth above the floor tom-tom. A clear resonant sound can be acquired by tuning the top heads to mid-range then tuning the bottom heads a minor third higher or major second.

2. If you want a clear but resonant muffled sound, adjust internal tone controls so pads almost touch the head.

3. If a live sound is desired on the bass drum in the set, tense the front head a little tighter than the one in back.

If a heavy loose effect used by todays "rock" groups is desired, do the following:

1. Tune the top head to bottom range and tune bottom head still lower. If you want more muffled quality you can tape a folded handkerchief that measures about two inches by two inches to the head away from the playing area on the head. If you want a heavy sound to the bass you can stuff it with paper or tape a heavy piece of flannel, terry or heavier material in a 4 by 5 inch pad on the inside of head. Ask your director to suggest the most desired sound and experiment. The sound desired is a low dull sound.

FOR THE MAXIMUM OF PROPER TUNING IN ALL PER-CUSSION INSTRUMENTS, TUNE CAREFULLY, CONSISTENTLY AND TAKE TIME.

Preventive Maintenance for Drums

1. Remove head and wipe off all dirt from both sides, in the counterhoop and on the inside of shell. Lubricate so heads move smoothly.

2. USE A CLEANING SOLVENT WITH CAUTION AROUND PLASTIC HEADS. IT WILL DISSOLVE THE FINISH OF THE WHITE COATING.

3. It is wiser to wash head with ivory liquid terry cloth dipped, and rung in soap/water solution. If heads are extremely dirty use an SOS pad very gently and rinse. Use a dampened cloth of soap

and water ONLY on Calfskin. Anything more will damage the head.

4. Clean rim with alcohol.

5. Don't write on heads or store near heat.

6. Never over-tension heads.

7. See that case or covers are on drums when not in use.

8. Check drum stand to see that it is solid and drums are properly locked in position.

FRENCH HORN TUNING

When tuning the double horn (Bb-F) tune the written F

1st valve on F horn and T on Bb horn and match

pitch. It is extremely important that the first and the second valves be tuned one step and a half step respectively below the open tones. This must coincide with both horns. The same must be true of the 2 and 3 valve combinations. See that horns are not tuned by percussion instruments or by a wall because of the distorted vibrations caused from such placement.

Trouble Shooting Maintenance

1. Check for frayed strings. Don't wait for string to break before restringing.

2. See that all slides are re-lubricated to work smoothly.

3. Check to see that all slides have been put in properly.

4. Check for dents in first eight inches of lead in pipe from mouthpiece.

5. The mouthpiece of the French Horn is more susceptible to acid damage than that of any other instrument and must be washed down and swabbed at least every two weeks.

6. Never stand a French Horn on its bell.

TUNING THE FLUTE AND PICCOLO

The head joint should not be fully inserted into its socket for standard pitch, but rather left out approximately the thickness of a nickel. If it is inserted all the way, it will cause the performer to play unbearably sharp.

Notes normally out of tune on all flutes and piccolos; High C#, Eb and F#. All are quite sharp and must be flatted by variations in the fingering or by humoring every time they are played.

Preventive Maintenance:

1. If a performer has difficulty playing the low tones on a flute there very likely may be a leaky pad. Bring this to the attention of your director.

2. Make sure a clean dry cloth is kept in every case for swabbing after playing, and that it covers the rod completely.

3. Tuning cork should be kept clean with a small amount of vaseline and the application of thin fresh cork grease.

4. Make sure that the tuning cork is pulled so that the mark on the tuning rod is exactly in the center of blow hole after cleaning.

5. Flute pads may stick to tone holes due to dirt, saliva or grease. Use pipe cleaner dampened with benzine and wipe pad clean. NEVER use alcohol because this will dry the skin.

6. Check for dents, loose keys, missing pads.

7. Are keys in good playing condition? Any metal pad washers missing?

8. See that piccolo or flutes are never laid on a chair while out of case.

TUNING THE OBOE

The length of reed and placement in the mouth are very critical. Generally we have found that an oboist making his own reeds and studying with a competent private instructor experiences less difficulty with intonation. Usually when the

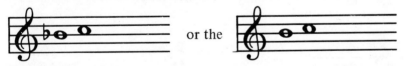

are wider apart than they should be, the oboist is playing with too much reed in the mouth. Also accompanying this problem will be sharpness in the high register and flatness in the low register.

Points to constantly check on when observing an oboist is:

1. Performer should blow into the oboe at the angle in which the instrument is held.

2. Make sure that the reed is supported fairly equally from all the sides.

3. You should not see any red part of the lips.

4. Watch the little finger. Have the player performer low D and check to see if he can reach any of the other keys without moving either the elbow or wrist.

Preventive Maintenance:

1. Especially common when checking oboe for cleanliness is the accumulation of dirt and grime in tone holes. Swab after every use and clean holes with pipe cleaner.

2. Avoid storing instrument in attic, basement or near radiator.

3. Use oil sparingly on keys.

4. Keep reeds in a container when not playing.

5. Never lay instrument on its keys.

6. Have at least two good reeds.

TUNING THE SAXOPHONE

The saxophones have a larger variance regarding pitch than the other woodwind instruments and it is therefore necessary to be more careful tuning them. Many players mark the location of the mouthpiece and believe to be in tune as long as they adhere to the mark. This can only be true when the room temperature and other variables are constant. Notes generally out of tune on the saxophone are:

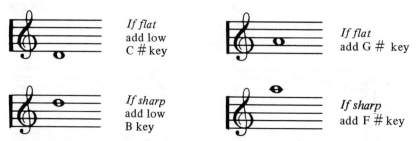

Maintenance of the Saxophone

1. Once a week wash mouthpiece cap and ligature in lukewarm water with a few drops of Ivory liquid soap.

2. REMEMBER, the saxophone is the most poorly cared for instrument in the woodwind family. Saliva acids cause chalky

deposits that cannot be removed with soap and water, so take extra care in maintaining high standards of cleanliness.

3. Swab out the inside of the body, bottom of horn and bell, daily.

4. Use a saxophone neck cleaner to keep the gooseneck clean and wash this neck with lukewarm water and Ivory liquid monthly.

5. Oil keys where they are attached to posts and where one key hinge moves against another but use oil VERY SPARINGLY because too much will collect dirt and lint. Work keys to distribute the oil. Preserve springs from rust with a thin coat of oil and give a touch up to screws that go through the heads of posts to lubricate and prevent rust.

6. Lubricate the cork on the gooseneck with cork grease at least weekly.

---

*Chart: Page 15 Selmer, "Bandwagon," No. 66, Oct. 1972. Copyright 1972, Selmer division of the Magnavox Company. Reproduced with permission.

CHAPTER 13

Gifted Students Tuning a Band

Music directors have an important job with seemingly insurmountable obstacles to overcome. That is why many directors have little time to teach student instructors or gifted student directors how to tune a band. One can improve the intonation of a band by using gifted students because the director then can walk around the room and measure intonation instead of relying only on the direction of sound aimed at the podium position. There are many questions that directors and student directors must ask before beginning. How does a band get in tune? How can we get it to stay in tune with each new note? How can we develop a band of listeners? What mistakes do we as directors make with our own ears? What instruments or tones play normally out of tune? Why do certain musical organizations consistently play in tune? How can we improve our ear?

Naturally there is little time to go around computing intervals nor do we have time to run around the room testing temperature and its effects on tuning. Somehow people get the misconception that if a director does these technicalities it helps. It may impress your Superintendent but it won't get the band in tune. What will help is SEEING a band or orchestra director who is noted for his fine in-tune musical organization actually tune a band. Suggestions for student instructors:

1. A video tape workshop of band directors "tuning" an Elementary or High School band or orchestra.

2. Charts made by the manufacturer with the year and brand of each instrument and what tones the instrument has a tendency to play out of tune.

3. *"Tuning The School Band and Orchestra"* by Dr. Ralph R. Pottle, 76 pages.

Now that the handy book is memorized, the student is ready for the first student. Ask, Do you know every instrument in the band or orchestra? Do you know which have a tendency to play sharp, which flat? Can you tell the student how to correct it? Do you know alternate fingerings to correct intonation? If you can do this, you're on the right road. If you don't know this, you've failed. Return to Chapter 12 and review each individual instrument. Then systematically get to know each instrument for sharp and flat tendencies. Does the student know his instrument well enough to tell you what tones play flat and sharp?

It is essential that a player know which tones on his instrument have a tendency to be out of tune and whether the tendency is sharp or flat. One way to determine this is to write out a chromatic scale for the complete range of the instrument, providing duplicate notes where there are several fingerings available. By tuning the instrument to a well tuned organ or piano or by using Stroboconn, he can match his notes to the equal-tempered scale of the instrument employed and mark with arrows the notes which are out of tune with this scale.

The arrows should point up if the note is sharp and down if flat. Longer arrows or some other device can be used to mark the notes which are more out of tune. The knowledge gained from this marked chromatic scale must be used in conjunction with listening while playing because playing in tune requires all players to match each other. This can be done only by listening and humming tones.

Anyone who has ever heard of the University of Michigan band marvels at the fine intonation. There is one method that the now retired William D. Revelli constantly stressed, "Think the note, sing the note, play the note." It is a useful method but the technical transmission of singing the note to the actual instrument note still possesses many problems.

Nilo Hovey, one time national band winner, has a series of ideas he found most helpful in getting an award winning band to play in tune. He suggests that the number one requirement is careful listening. If we are to encourage careful listening as a habit, we must start with materials that will permit discrimination. The student who cannot play a sustained note in tune will certainly not play in tune when concentrating on speed. Naturally each student must know the characteristics of his instrument. For example, attention must be given to flatness of the 5th partial in brasses, sharpness of certain valve combinations. Each student must know the methods of favoring the pitch upward and downward—manipulation of embouchure, oral cavity, breath support, direction of air column, etc.

A warning to all string players: Tuning the open strings of the violins does not insure good intonation. Tuning problems of the band would be greatly simplified if we could tune to a single unison tone—say Concert Bb—and let this suffice. Unfortunately it is not that easy. Students must be taught to *"hear"* the harmonic intervals, for a good portion of their group playing involves these intervals. Chord playing can be an aid to better intonation.

Figure 5

**Using a gifted student to
direct and tune a band**

PYRAMID METHOD OF TUNING

Among the main ear-training devices are the following:

1. A unison (octave) scale in moderate range.

2. Octave pyramids, especially low to high, grouping sections as follows:

Bass Clarinet	Bassoon	Bb Clarinet	Piccolo
Contrabass Cl.	Alto Clar.	Alto Sax	Flute
Baritone Sax	Tenor Sax	Cornet	Eb Clar.
String Bass	Horn	Trumpet	Oboe
Tuba	Trombone		
	Baritone		

3. Comparison of any section to any other section or combination.

4. Playing a common chord sequence tutti.

5. Varying the entrance of one or more sections with a unison note.

6. Hearing pitch level as set by Tubas, Baritones, Trombones, then adding sections, one at a time.

7. Testing the arpeggio by one player or a section against Chord of full band.

8. Separating root, 3rd and 5th of chords for more minute checking.

9. Selecting 1st chair players (and other combinations) for further checking.

10. Changing chords by lowering 3rd of major, raising 3rd of minor, raising 5th of major, lowering root of major, etc. to focus attention on the moving part.

AUTHOR'S METHOD FOR TUNING A BAND

Although every director has his special means of tuning, the following works and can be taught easily to a gifted student director:

1. Tune instruments one to another from each side of the band i.e. conductor's left, conductor's right, front of band, back of band. In this manner, students hear pitch better.

2. Sustain concert Bb with basses and lowest woodwinds. Continue to add instruments in order of range, and tune in octaves.

3. Place electro tuner in back of band and tune each instrument individually to tuner. Students hear out of tune vibrations easier this way. Leave the snare tension on the drums in order that out-of-tune vibrations can be amplified sympathetically.

4. When students are not sensitive to pitch, tune to strobotuner and the director's ear.

5. After the band is in tune to concert Bb play chords in whole notes, and place a fermata on chord tone. Repeat same chord, placing fermata on other chord tone until possibilities are exhausted. Band works on tuning sustained tone through *"humoring"* pitch.

6. Tune one section to another.

7. Locate out-of-tune chord. Start with lowest chord tone (sustained) and continue adding sustained tones until out-of-tune voice is located.

It is important to impress on the student that every note is a tuning note, especially the long notes. Tuning is a full time job and must be mandatory at every rehearsal.

THE STROBOSCOPE

Over the years the music companies have done their best to develop mechanical devices to aid the director in tuning a band. One of these devices is the stroboscope. There are many pros and cons to using this instrument as it is an excellent visual aid and a fine point of departure. A far superior way to test pitch is to listen and correct the beats which are produced when playing in unison. Improve intonation through practice of refining those beats usually caused by imperfect unisons.

TUNING BAR AND PIANO METHOD

Specific Ear-Training for Students

Along with listening to chords a method that has been successful is to play intervals on the piano and have students identify them in a general way as 3rds, 4ths, 5ths not a minor third or major third or perfect 4th etc. Once they begin to identify intervals either by testing each other by humming or singing intervals, students become more interested in the accurate tuning of these intervals. During rehearsals, when an instrument or instruments are out of tune, stop rehearsal and have the out of tune instrument sustain the notes. Students' facial expressions indicate approval when notes are played in tune.

When tuning with a tuning bar sound have the instrument play and ask anyone in the band whether it is in tune or out of tune. This eliminates day dreaming and makes students responsible for listening. As this skill improves send the section leaders out of the room down the hall at least 150 feet and ask them to listen to the band perform and give their critical evaluation on tuning and tone quality. This will accomplish more than the gifted director can because comments are from the peer group.

When performing for the section leaders who are out in the hall, be sure to select a slow chorale or something that the ear can easily identify regarding pitch and tone quality.

This is especially important as most fast music sounds acceptable to the untrained ear. RULE: ALL NOTES ARE TUNING NOTES ESPECIALLY THE LONG NOTES.

Another technique is to assign groups of instruments the root 3rd and the 5th of the chord. Instruct all students that they will be playing chromatically ascending or descending. The right hand will indicate the voice that is root 3rd or 5th. The left hand will indicate whether the voice is to go chromatically up or down.

All instruments are to sustain notes unless instructed by the conductor to change chromatically. This technique is a good substitute for the chorale warm-up because it keeps students and director on their mental toes. Students are forced to think chromatically and the conductor is unlimited in the chord possibilities he can structure. The following benefits are derived from this chromatic warm-up approach:

1. Long tones to improve tone and tuning.
2. Knowledge of chromatic.
3. Tuning to other voices while playing either root, 3rd or 5 of chord (depending on how conductor structures chords).
4. Good warm-up technique, it sets the stage for serious concentration from the onset.

VIDEO TAPING

Encourage Band or Orchestra Parents' Organizations to purchase a video tape machine as part of their budget expenditures.

Not only will it improve the band quality but it can be used by gifted student directors during rehearsals.

Most directors during the course of a school year are required to be away from classes for conventions, business or sickness. During this time, gifted students can benefit by taking over a band rehearsal. Usually the procedure is to acquire a certified substitute teacher who is not able to direct musical groups. The substitute supervises the room and the gifted student-director conducts the rehearsal. This avoids band, choir or orchestra rehearsal periods being turned into a study hall.

Teach gifted student directors to direct a band during regular rehearsals. Correct, compliment and criticize his work outside of band time. Insist that without the director's presence the video tape be on so that the attitude of the band and the techniques of the gifted director are studied. Several student directors should be capable of directing the band at any one time.

Upon return, the director need not be discouraged with wasted hours and the video tape also reveals potential problems within the organization. This technique will also discourage a large group from getting out of hand. The student directors' technique under independence and stress can also be studied.

TEACHING THE SMALLER ENSEMBLE

During solo contest many teachers spend hours listening to ensembles prepare for contest. The percentage of time spent doing this can be greatly decreased if the music director will completely turn over the ensemble direction to individual students. The director should be used for repertoire lists of ensemble material and as an aid to correct special technical and interpretive problems. Each ensemble should be heard at least once, preferably twice before contest.

There is nothing more gratifying than seeing a student teacher's extreme pleasure after acquiring a first division rating for his or her ensemble. It is most rewarding because that student knows he accomplished this by himself.

Students can acquire knowledge of directing at a rapid rate. They may work with the group in their own home and can analyze discrepancies. These discrepancies can be discussed with the music director after a rehearsal. Usually the invitation to hear each

Figure 6
**Gifted student working with small
ensemble in preparation for contest**

ensemble should be held open. Each *gifted director* should seek
assistance on his own.

Music directors may be reluctant to delegate directing responsi-
bilities to gifted students because sweepstakes points are at stake.
However, losing an ensemble contest is also an education. Handing
over the reins to a gifted student director is no easy decision but
one that can be truly rewarding. Many a gifted student director is
capable and many more can be with patient intervention rather
than complete direction from the music teacher. This approach
must be carefully supervised for maximum results. Poor supervision is sure failure. Only upper classmen should be considered
for these assignments.

CHAPTER 14

Awareness of Deceptiveness
in Intonation
for the Gifted Music Student

Because of the highly technical aspect of intonation and its relation to temperature, gifted music students may find education in this area amiss or non-existent. That is why an abbreviated study in this area is presented. Although the aspects of this chapter are quite technical they can be understood easily with a little concentration on the part of the student. Temperature must be understood as crucial to proper intonation on any musical organization large or small; therefore, no matter how carefully you tune a band or how carefully your students listen to the director, they must understand and be aware of the villain called temperature.

TEMPERATURE CHANGES AND ITS EFFECTS

In 1939 an International Tuning Standard of A-440 cycles per second at 72° F was adopted.

Any tuning standard that is adopted must be defined in terms of a definite temperature. This is true in wind instruments because the speed of sound in air changes with temperature. Wind instruments become sharper if the speed of sound is faster, and they become flatter if it is slower. Since the speed of sound increases with higher temperatures, the sound goes through the instrument faster, and the instrument is sharper, because effectively, it is shorter. On the other hand, mallet-played instruments tend to become slightly flatter with change of temperature because of the expansion of the bar material with higher temperatures.

TRADITIONAL STANDARDS AND
INTERNAL-EXTERNAL TEMPERATURES

Tuning standards traditionally have been set at the environmental temperature. However, wind instruments are sensitive to two temperature influences—that of the environment, or external temperature, and that of the player's breath. The temperature inside the instrument, the internal temperature, lies somewhere between that of the breath and that of the environment. The internal temperature changes with the type of music since the instrument actually becomes warmer with legato passages where the player's breath is more sustained in the instrument. All research in the field of the effect of temperature on wind instruments has indicated that because of the two temperature factors involved, smaller instruments do not vary as widely with external temperature as do the large instruments, but even those smaller instruments do not vary to the same degree. Some small disagreement exists between different measurements that have been obtained in the field because of the method of combination of the two types of temperature factors.

BREATH EFFECTS

Since the effect of the player's breath is present, it is important that all wind instruments be played and warmed thoroughly with the breath before tuning.

The practice of many professional flutists who actually blow air through the instrument with the lips covering the embouchure hole is one evidence of thorough warming before playing. Brass basses are affected by change in external temperature more than any other instrument because the player's breath has relatively less effect upon the temperature of the instrument and it takes longer for the internal temperature to stabilize. Actually in laboratory experiments, at temperatures less than 80°, fifteen to twenty minutes of playing a brass bass has been necessary in order to stabilize intonation. If the external temperature varies, the brass basses should be checked fairly often and readjusted to a standard tuning. For instance, a rise in temperature, which is so common during a performance on the concert stage, may cause the basses to become sharp, which in turn tends to cause everyone in the organization to adjust *"toward the sharp side,"* with consequent intonation problems. The bright lights required by television accentuate this problem. Just to warm an instrument thoroughly before tuning is not sufficient. During a long rest in the performance, any wind instrument should be warmed by blowing the breath through the instrument to avoid flatness when playing is resumed.

STATISTICAL STANDARDS

A common question is, What standard should be used if the temperature is higher than 72°? If wind instruments are used in conjunction with mallet-played instruments, or piano, it is desirable to adjust the winds so that they can be played at the same tuning level as the non-winds. If extreme adjustment is necessary, intonation difficulty in the winds can be expected. Dance band musicians, who often have to play with pianos that are tuned with "A" lower than 440 cps, have great difficulty with intonation because of this fact. A knowledge of the effect of temperature on any particular instrument can be helpful to aid in the adjustment that the ear demands.

If only wind instruments are used in the ensemble, then to some degree the tuning standard should be allowed to rise as the temperature rises. This will allow performance with a minimum of tuning adjustments. However, since each instrument changes differently with external temperature, some suitable compromise standard must be adopted. The clarinet, because of the disparity in distance from the reed, first tone holes and bell tones, has a minimum of latitude in tuning. It plays a prominent role in the wind ensemble and has much to recommend it as the tuning standard for such a group. Its length and physical characteristics are such that it warms quite quickly with the player's breath, and once warmed, changes less with external temperature. Using the clarinet as a tuning standard, if no non-wind instruments are present, a useful rule of thumb could be formulated thus: *"The frequency of the tuning standard may be permitted to rise approximately one double vibration (cycle) for each ten degrees rise in temperature."*

This approximation, A=440 cps at 72°F., 441 at 80°F. (+4 cents). 1 442 at 90°F. (+8 cents), and 443 at 100° F. (+12 cents), will come close to following the rise of the flute and clarinet. Thus, extreme variation because of tuning adjustments of these instruments will be avoided. Such an adjustment would greatly lessen the amount of tuning slide pull needed by the larger brass instruments, and the lower woodwinds would not require an extreme adjustment. If A=440 were maintained in spite of higher temperature, the lower woodwinds in particular would have drastic intonation problems.

COURSE OF ACTION

It becomes apparent that several courses of action are available to the director. If the temperature is near 72°F., wind instruments conforming with the International Tuning Standard can be easily adjusted to the non-wind instruments and all is well. However, suppose the temperature is 80° or over, and the score calls for orchestra bells and piano. If the bell tones of the clarinet are used for tuning down to A=440 cps to correspond to the non-wind instruments, the throat tones of the clarinet will be miserably flat and their quality will suffer. Thus, in tuning down to A-440 when room temperatures are higher, it is very important that several representative notes be checked rather than a single tuning note. Ideally, the instrument should be adjusted until the number and amount of sharp tones would balance the number and amount of flat tones. By avoiding extremes, the experienced player can more nearly humor the out-of-tune notes sufficiently to correct their intonation. If the temperature approaches 100°F., the director is faced with a dilemma when non-wind instruments are to be used with the wind ensemble. In such a case, satisfactory internal intonation cannot be achieved among the winds if adjustment is made to A-440. The upper register of all the woodwinds becomes relatively very flat, as do all tones emanating from the upper tone holes. The brass basses have insufficient slide pull available.

SUMMATION

In summary—the conductor may permit the tuning standard to move sharp enough at higher temperatures to permit the wind instruments to have satisfactory internal intonation. In this case he must "live with" the discrepancy between the winds and non-winds. On the other hand he can remedy the wind-non-wind discrepancy and maintain approximately an A-440 standard regardless of temperature. In that event he must *"live with"* the resulting problems of internal tuning of the wind instruments. An indiscriminate, completely uncontrolled change in pitch with temperature is to be avoided no matter what choice is made.

EAR POLLUTION

The greatest enemy to a musical organization is ear pollution. Recently a doctor stated that our noses should be replaced by mechanical devices because they no longer function as a warning signal. If you were to drive about hundred miles away from a large city, turn around and drive back it would be easy to see the thick layer of black smog. It would be easy to smell the sulphur and obnoxious odors, but remaining in this environment for a length of time we cease recognizing these offensive smells. The same phenomena happens to our ears musically. As long as we are in the audience listening to someone else's organization, we can be most critical. Place us in the middle of our own band or orchestra and, after a few minutes, we TUNE OUT. Sometimes a gifted student-director won't be aware that he is doing just that. This is the ultimate danger, until it is brought to his attention. Ask how the solo flute player is handling a difficult passage. Then ask how the second chair flute is handling the passage. One can become so entranced with the lovely melody that one tunes out the second chair section.

One of the best ways to become aware of the tricks the ears can play is to actually know what the technical things are that happen to the ear. It seems that most instrumental music directors rely heavily upon intuitive sense in their teaching and conducting of performing groups. A certain degree of this sensitivity is necessary and desirable, but by combining the intuitive with the scientific it is apparent that more beneficial results are possible. Do you really understand what happens to sound in loudness and distance?

1. Sound naturally falls off gradually with distance but loudness does not decrease so quickly. It is therefore important that total harmony is carried in the brasses and that the woodwinds be given unison passages in the upper range.

2. In lower frequencies, a tone must be louder to sound equal in loudness to a much higher tone. Louder tones must be produced in the lower register to achieve dynamic consistency.

3. A crescendo must be faster in the beginning and gradually decreased in speed as it becomes louder.

4. Since the human ear discriminates loudness levels much better at higher frequencies, the lower instruments must give more noticeable dynamics while the upper instruments use the fine sensitivity with a gradation of volume.

5. The ear is much less sensitive to differences in pitch that are low in tone. It is also less sensitive to softer tones. Your intonation problems are less noticeable in low instruments when they are played softly.

One doesn't have to look far to run into so many technical problems with intonation that the director becomes almost terrified to rely on anything, much less using a gifted student-director to tune a band. That is why one must constantly test and retest the most important instrument of all, the human ear. Practical aids are the tuning bar, electro tuner, strobotuner or stroboconn and a tuning fork. Use them!

Take your student-director's ear out to a professional concert, opera or professional recording. Never trust the ear, refresh it by treating it. Note the contrast of hearing a professional concert one evening then tuning up a band or orchestra the next morning. The contrast should be quite different.

The ears are magnificent precision instruments. Treat them badly and they will deteriorate. Train, educate and challenge them day after day, and you will be amazed at the computerized speed and sensitivity with which they learn to react to the slightest imperfection in intonation. Keep training and retraining your ear along with the gifted student. Keep your ears sharpened and honed by devoting a portion of each day's practice time to the study of intonation. Ear pollution can be avoided.

The information on temperature is from "The Effect of Temperature on Tuning Standards of Wind Instruments" by Jody C. Hall and Earle L. Kent, reprinted through the courtesy of C.G. Conn Ltd.

Index

A

Academic Achievement, 24
Acceptance, 23
Achievement, 20
    arithmetic, 20
    language, 20
Action in tuning, 201
Activities, 26
    athletic, 26
    extra curricular, 26
    social, 26
Adaptability, 159
Adjustment, 23
Administrative Questions, 87, 88
Analyzation of gifted, 34-46
Application form, 89
    private instructor, 90, 91
Architects, 119
Articulation, 170
    high school, 172, 173
Arts
    guidelines, 129, 130
    lectures, 133
    notebook, 128, 129
    outline sheets, 130, 133
    record lists, 134-138
Author's method
    tuning, 193, 194
Authoritarian role, 164
Anxiety, 26
    high-anxious, 26
    low-anxious, 26

B

Ban visitation, 175, 176
Baritones, 180
    tune, 180
Baroque records, 135
Bass drum tune, 184

Basses tune, 180, 181
Bassoon
    maintenance, 182
    reeds, 181, 182
    tune, 181, 182
Behaviorial objectives, 76
Blues guitar, 148, 149
Bongos tune, 184
Boogie Woogie, 146
Book practical value, 7
Book, tuning, 191
Booklist, halftime, 52-54
Brain child, 49
Brainstorming, 52
Breath effects, 199
Broadway hits guitar, 147

C

Careful listening, 192
Cassettes for testing, 154, 155
Catalogues, halftime, 55
20th Century records, 138
Changing chords tuning, 193
Character analysis, 158
Characteristics, 19
Chart
    expectancy grid, 43
    I.Q., 92
    Rand-difference correlation, 45
    Scattergram, 44
    Statistical Rank, 41
    Tally Farnum, 92
    Torrance, 92
Chart analyzation, 37
    Expectancy grid, 37
    Farnum, 37
    I.Q., 37
    Scattergram, 37
    Statistical breakdown, 37
    Torrance, 37

Chart preparation, 34-36
Chart I.Q., 35, 36
Chart I.Q. and Performance, 36
Charts, tuning, 191
Charting, 173
Chord playing, 192
Chromatic, 194
Citizenship, 159
Clarinet maintenance, 183
Clarinet tune, 182, 183
Classical guitar, 147
Classicism records, 135, 136
Club Request Form, 84, 85
College culmination, 23
College Songs guitar, 146
Color combinations, 52
Common Chord tuning, 193
Comparative Arts, 117-138
Compassion, 160
Compatability, 159
Composers, 119, 120
Computing intervals, 190
Concert Bb tune, 192
Concert feedback, 95
Conga tune, 184
Continuance student teacher, 167, 168
Controls for gifted, 161-176
Cooperation, 159
Cornets tune, 180, 181
Correlations
    achievement and creativity, 22
    I.Q.-Creativity, 22
    linear, 22
Country guitar, 148, 149
Creativity vs. achievement, 21
Creativity student teacher, 157
Crescendo, 203
Critical analysis material, 78
Critical critiques, 114-116
Curriculum handbook description, 88

D

Deception intonation, 198-203
Dedication, 158
Definition, 20
    folk-jazz, 83
Direction teaching, 110, 111
Director's ear, 180
Discipline, 26
Discrimination, 192
Dismissal, 175
Discipline, strict, 26
Distance loudness, 202
Distintive characteristics
    gifted-creative, 19-29

Dramatists, 120, 121
Drum
    maintanance, 185, 186
    tune, 183, 184
    sets tune, 185
Duration, 56

E

Ear
    books, 111
    materials, 111
    pollution, 202
    precision instruments, 203
    sensitivity, 202
    training, 111, 113
    tricks, 202
Easy Way to Guitar, 145
Effects of temperature tuning, 198, 199
Electro tuner, 194
Enthusiasm, 158
Ethnomusicology
    booklist, 97, 98
    films, 97
    magazines, 96
    records, 96
    sourcebook, 98
Evaluation student teacher, 167
Expectancy Grid, 35-37
Explanatory role, 164
Expressive skills, 156, 157
External temperature, 199

F

Favoring pitch, 192
Feeder schools, 170, 171
Fees, 166
Fermata, 194
First chair players tuning, 193
Flatness tune, 192
Flute
    maintenance, 187
    tune, 186, 187
Folk definition, 83
Folk guitar, 148, 149
Folk-Jazz, 82-98
Footnotes, 28, 29
Form, 156
French horn
    maintenance, 186
    tune, 186
Fund raising
    distributors, 93-95
    projects, 92, 93

G

Gifted leader's ear, 180
Good elaborators, 25
Gospel definition, 84
Gossip, 174
Grades, 25
Guitar, 139, 149
    arrangements, 146
    cassettes, 144
    filmstrips, 143
    method, 142
    method books, 144
    question sheet, 140, 141

H

Halftime
    checklist, 65
    editing production, 64
    evaluation, 63
    flash, 57, 58
    guidelines, 60
    shows, 49-65
    video tape analysis, 64
    worksheet, 61-63
Harmony, 156
    in basses, 202
High School Feeder, 171, 172
    rank, 21
Home-bound students, 162

I

Identification, 19
Imitation, 176
Improvement student teacher, 168, 169
Improvisational guitar, 149
Individual analyzation, 38
    psychological, 39, 40
Individualized programs, gifted, 49-149
Inferiority feelings, 23
Instant Fun Guitar, 145
Instructional objectives, 73
Instructor selection, 88, 89
Instruments
    one other tuning, 193
    sharpness, 198
    Stroboconn, 191
    tune organ, 191
    tune piano, 191
Integrity, 158
Internal temperature, 199
International tuning standard, 198
Intonation, 198
Introduction to Music, 141, 142
Inventions, 123-128

I

I.Q., 19
    plateau, 20
Isolating gifted, 139

J

Jazz definition, 83
Jobbing musician, 113
Judge, 176
Jury, 176

K

Know instruments, 191

L

Lack of interest, 175
    responsibility, 174
Logic role, 164
Long notes tuning, 195
Low tones, 203
Lower frequencies, 203
Lower instrument dynamics, 203

M

Magna-board use, 51
Magno-Men supplies, 58
Mail, 176
Mallets and temperature, 199
Manipulation of embouchure, 192
Marching time table, 57
Marked chromatic scale, 191
Master Theory Books, 100, 103
Materials, 50, 51
Measurement, 19
Medieval records, 134
Melody, 155
Minnesota test results, 102
Multi-media approach, 66-81
Music Appreciation, 66-81
    chart analysis, 72
    charts, 71
    tape production, 69
Musicgraphs, 71
Music List, 55, 56
Music Theory, 99-116

N

New Guitar Course, 145
Novelists, 120, 121

O

Oboe
    maintenance, 188
    tuning, 187, 188
Observation tuning, 190
Octave pyramids tuning, 193
Open strings, 192
Opera, 203
Organizational ability, 159
Original thinkers, 25
Overachievers, 22
Overviewing, 117

P

Painters, 121, 122
Para-professional compensation, 92
Parental
    background, 25
    feedback, 175
Participation form, 86, 87
Personality
    traits, 24
    types, 24
Piano tuning, 195
Piccolo
    maintenance, 187
    tune, 186, 187
Pilot Course Form, 86
Pitfalls, 82, 83
Podium position, 190
Poets, 120, 121
Private instructors list, 173
Private lessons, 173, 174
Problems, student teacher, 174
Productivity, 22, 23
Professional
    concerts, 203
    records, 203
Progress reports, 165, 166
Projects, 25
Prudence, 174
Psychological encouragement, 51
Pyramid tuning, 193

Q

Questioning specifics, 164
Questionnaire, 170, 171

R

Rank - difference correlation, 22
Rap sessions, 113
Reading preferences, 26, 27

Religious guitar, 146
Renaissance records, 134
Responsibility, 158, 159
Retraining ears, 203
Rhythm, 155
Rhythmic accuracy, 153
Risk situations, 24
Rock guitar, 148, 149
Role playing, 163, 164
Romanticism records, 136, 137
Rutgers Dictation Series, 111, 113

S

Safety guide, 139
Saxophone
    maintenance, 188, 189
    tune, 188
SCAT test, 21
Scattergram, 35, 36
    chart, 37
Scheduling, 49, 50
Scholastic aptitude, 28
Script
    presentation, 75
    sample, 75, 76, 77
Sculptors, 122, 123
Section tuning, 193
Selecting arts figures, 118
Self directed evaluation, 162
    learning, 161
    programs, 153
Sense of Humor, 27, 28
Sharp/flat tendencies, 191
Sharpness tune, 192
Sight reading, 153
Sing-a-long-folk guitar, 146
Sing/play notes, 191
Single horns tune, 180, 181
Slide
    preparation, 72, 73
    script, tape coordination, 77, 78
    set-up, 73, 74
Slide and electric guitar, 147
Smaller ensemble, 196, 197
Snare drum tuning, 184
Sociability, 25
Socioeconomic
    level, 25
    status, 21
Solo contest, 196
Soul, definition, 89
Soul guitar, 147
Spanish guitar, 147
Speed of sound tuning, 198
Statistical rank breakdown, 37

Status, 23
Stroboscope, 194
Strobotuner, 194
Student
    feedback, 175
    handbook, 178-189
    preparedness list, 155-157
    teachers, 153-160
Supplemental study, 113
Suppliers List
    half-time, 58
Sustain Bb tuning, 193
Sustained chords tuning, 194
Sweepstake points, 197

T

Tally of Farnum, 37
Tape
    carrel use, 67-69
    fanfares, 60
    making, 69-70
    recording, 59
    worksheets, 70, 71
Technical Manual, 30, 31
Technique, 153
Telephone, 175
Telescopic Curriculum, 66, 67
Television and temperature, 200
Temperature
    brass, 199, 200
    summation 200, 201
Temperament, 24
Terminal Behavior test, 77
Tests
    cost, 30
    creative, 30
    grading, 32
    median, 32
    music theory students, 102-108
    non-theory students, 101, 102
    self-scoring
    "T" scores
    theory and harmony, 109, 110
    Torrance, 30
Testing
    arpeggio, 193
    dialogue, 31, 32
    entering behavior, 99, 100
    gifted, 30-34
    procedure, 31
Third, fifth chord tuning, 193

Timbales tune, 184
Timpani tune, 184
Tone color, 156
Tone quality, 153
Torrance test, 30, 33, 39
Trouble areas, 180
Trouble maintenance, 181
Tune band, 178
Tuning
    band, 190-197
    bar, 194, 195
    fork, 203
    group instruments, 177
    instruments, 177-189
    notes, 194
    organ, 177
    out, 202
    piano, 117
    sections, 178, 180
    Stroboconn, 177
    variables, 180
Tune band, 178

U

Underachievers, 22, 23, 24
Unison scale tuning, 193
Using
    second chair flute, 202
    solo flute, 202

V

Verbal questioning, 20
Video tape use, 95, 96
    in tuning, 190
Vocation
    clerical, 24
    managerial, 24
    professional fathers, 24
    semi-skilled, 24
    skilled, 24

W

Warming instrument, 199
Wind instrument temperature, 200, 201
World events, 123-128
Worksheet, 79, 80
    analysis, writing, 79, 80
    book review, 78
    book review checklist, 81
Written critiques, 114